D1055182

Biz Dev Done Right Endorsements

"I have witnessed thousands of well-meaning companies get business development wrong. In Biz Dev Done Right, Caryn and Carl point out the critical blind spots in sales that you need to know to be successful. If you're looking to scale up profitable revenue, read this book!"

—**Verne Harnish**, founder of the *Entrepreneurs' Organization* (EO), CEO of *Gazelles*, and author of *Scaling Up (Rockefeller Habits 2.0)* and *The Greatest Business Decisions of All Time*

"If you are looking to make more money with less work, then read this book now! You'll learn not only how to fill your pipeline with solid leads but also how to convert them to sales, all while exceeding the customer's needs. WOW! Business owners/CEOs, sales managers, and sales professionals, Biz Dev Done Right is truly the shortcut to success."

—**Jack Daly**, serial entrepreneur and author of *Hyper Sales Growth*

"When companies get business development right, there is no limit to their success. In their book, Biz Dev Done Right, Caryn and Carl provide secrets for success. The practical tips and ideas in this book will put you on the shortest path to getting business development done right. I recommend it for all who want to hire and retain the best people possible and achieve significant business growth."

—**Marsha Firestone**, Ph.D., founder and president, *Women Presidents' Organization*

"Congratulations Caryn and Carl on writing the book that every CEO, sales manager, and sales professional needs to read if they want to achieve next level growth. Business development is a complex and frustrating topic for so many, and they have distilled this into a simple and pragmatic format that everyone can follow."

—**Monica S. Smiley**, publisher/CEO, *Enterprising Women* magazine

"*Business development can be as mystical as marketing—and identifying the exact efforts that yield results can be just as tricky. But no longer! Kopp and Gould have created the playbook we've all been waiting for! Read this book now!*"

—**Christine Comaford**, neuroscience-based growth coach, serial entrepreneur, *NY Times* bestselling author of *SmartTribes: How Teams Become Brilliant Together*

"*Caryn Kopp knows more than most of us ever will about cold calling and business development. Lucky for all of us she has an ability to distill decades of ingenuity into easy, practical steps that result in increased sales. Whew.*"

—**Christina Harbridge**, mischief executive officer, *Allegory, Inc.*

"*I have been a professional speaker, executive speech coach, Speaker School producer and Vistage speaker and chair for decades. In working with business owners in so many different capacities, one challenge remains constant ... how to increase sales? Along came Caryn Kopp! If you want to know what strategies work and don't work, you need this book! If you want to get it right without making costly mistakes, you need this book! Every business owner looking for growth needs to read this book ... and if you're not, why are you in business?*"

—**Mikki Williams**, CSP, CPAE, professional speaker/ executive speech coach/*Vistage* speaker and chair

"*If you're serious about new business development and growing your business, then this book is a must. It is practical, insightful, and filled with actionable advice that you can implement immediately. This book was written for people who want real-world advice and not just theory. When we are faced with sales challenges, we often ask ourselves, 'What would Caryn do?'*"

—**Larry Cohen**, CEO, *Axis Promotions*

"*Biz Dev Done Right uncovers the often uncomfortable truths that business owners and sales leaders need to address. But it doesn't stop there—this book will make you think about things that may not be obvious. Then, in plain and clear language, you'll learn exactly what steps to take in order to succeed. Large and small companies alike can benefit from this advice.*"

—**Frank Minishak**, VP Agency Development, *Rocket Fuel*

"*For the past 18 years, I have worked with many speakers and consultants who all 'say' their book is different. This book is different because it listens to the salesperson and goes to the core of who they are as people. It highlights their strengths and is compassionate toward their weakness. It identifies solutions to build a stronger path to successful sales. Caryn Kopp has presented, "The Path to the Cash!" to my YPO Global One members. Caryn's suggestions were spot on and helped members build more connected sales teams and processes. Biz Dev Done Right goes directly into her secrets and methods. You will get a lot out of this personally and professionally.*"

—**Samantha Borland**, *YPO Global One*, chapter director

"*If you are a business owner, sales VP, or seller whose business has reached a plateau you can't get over, read this book now. It will help you identify what is keeping you from greater sales success and show you course corrections that will take you to the next level.*"

—**Alice R. Heiman**,
founder and chief sales officer of *Alice Heiman, LLC*

BIZ
DEV
DONE
RIGHT

BIZ DEV DONE RIGHT

DEMYSTIFYING THE **SALES PROCESS**
AND ACHIEVING THE REUSLTS YOU WANT

BY **CARYN KOPP** | Chief Door Opener®
& **CARL GOULD** | Chief DISCoverY Officer™

658.85
Kop

Published by Advantage, Charleston, South Carolina.
Member of Advantage Media Group.

ADVANTAGE is a registered trademark and the Advantage colophon is a trademark of Advantage Media Group, Inc.

Printed in the United States of America.

ISBN: 978-1-59932-679-5
LCCN: 2015946891

This publication is designed to provide accurate and authoritative information in regard to the subject matter covered. It is sold with the understanding that the publisher is not engaged in rendering legal, accounting, or other professional services. If legal advice or other expert assistance is required, the services of a competent professional person should be sought.

Advantage Media Group is proud to be a part of the Tree Neutral® program. Tree Neutral offsets the number of trees consumed in the production and printing of this book by taking proactive steps such as planting trees in direct proportion to the number of trees used to print books. To learn more about Tree Neutral, please visit **www.treeneutral.com**. To learn more about Advantage's commitment to being a responsible steward of the environment, please visit **www.advantagefamily.com/green**

Advantage Media Group is a publisher of business, self-improvement, and professional development books and online learning. We help entrepreneurs, business leaders, and professionals share their Stories, Passion, and Knowledge to help others Learn & Grow. Do you have a manuscript or book idea that you would like us to consider for publishing? Please visit **advantagefamily.com** or call **1.866.775.1696.**

ACKNOWLEDGMENTS

From Carl Gould

First, I want to thank my co-author Caryn Kopp who provided brilliant content, challenged my assumptions, and gave amazing insights to this book. I feel like I learned as much as I shared in this process! To the coaches, mentors, and consultants at 7 Stage Advisors, thank you for taking these methodologies into organizations and showing them how to accelerate their business (and personal) growth. You are the top advisory team in the world, and I am grateful that I get a ringside seat! To my beautiful wife Chandra and my kids, who supported me (okay, well tolerated …) during the late nights, early mornings, and weekends while Caryn and I created and refined this book. And lastly, to all of you business development professionals out there, you rainmakers, that dare to share your products and services with the world; you are the inspiration and motivation for this work. You are trying to change the world through your efforts, and we want to help you get there!

From Caryn Kopp

Thank you to my husband Doug (one of the best business developers I know, who can turn a prospect's "no" into a "yes" and then triple the size of the sale) and my children Jamie and Jason, my shining stars, who patiently supported me through the weekends, early mornings, and late nights it took to write this book while I also ran a growing business. Thank you to my team at Kopp Consulting, the most elite group of creative, intuitive sellers and support staff who constantly impress me and who make our clients' business development dreams come true. They literally take our clients where they've never been before! I learn something new from them every day. Finally, thank you to my co-author, Carl, who feels as strongly as I do that business owners, sales VPs, and sellers don't need to waste time and money or miss opportunities. There is a more direct Path To The Cash! All the hours of collaboration it took us to transfer what was in our heads onto paper will help so many businesses get business development done right.

TABLE OF CONTENTS

INTRODUCTION

Not long ago, my husband and I took our two teenagers to Laguna Cliffs, California. The trip was for my birthday, so I got to pick the activity: bike riding along the gorgeous Southern California coast. Now, my family would have probably preferred to lounge on the beach, but I coaxed them onto their bikes with the promise of a delicious breakfast on the San Clemente pier after the first leg of our ride. We set out as the sun rose over the mountains to the east, the ocean sparkling to our right.

The pier was about an hour away by bike, but—as I reminded my sleepy companions—a legendary breakfast with a beautiful view awaited us! After about 45 minutes, we reached a fork in the road. There was no sign indicating which path led directly to the pier. Both paths looked like they hugged the coast, so it was impossible to tell which one led to our destination. After a brief water break, we made our best guess and plowed forward.

As it turned out, the road we selected did take us to the pier. But instead of riding just 15 more minutes from the fork, the trip took nearly 45 minutes. When we chose the path, we couldn't see that it was full of sharp uphill climbs, as well as many twists and turns. Sweaty, dehydrated, exhausted, and starving, we did finally get our pancakes, but no one was feeling happy to be there!

Sometimes, growing a business can be a bit like biking an unfamiliar trail. You're moving forward, but you can't escape the feeling that you're exerting way more energy than you need to. When you arrive at your various milestones, you know in your gut that you should have gotten there a long time ago. And you can't help wondering how many opportunities you're missing along the way.

In our case, by the time our mistake at the fork became obvious, we didn't even consider turning back, because we had already invested so much time and energy into the path we chose. After speaking to some locals at breakfast, we learned that had we chosen the other path, we would have found a small road along the beach that would have brought us to the pier quickly. Had we only taken the time to ask for help with our decision, we could have been eating our pancakes much sooner.

The journey of any growing business is full of forks in the road, as well as many unexpected twists and turns. If only business owners, sales VPs, and sellers had someone to ask which paths were right, they could avoid the ones that were wrong. If only they knew what their blind spots were within the sales process, they could fix them and get business development done right.

For over 17 years, my company has been helping clients find new clients. My team and I have successfully advised thousands of business leaders, ensuring that they get in front of the prospects they have been seeking for so long. Through our Door Opener® Service, we get our clients the initial meetings with key decision makers that put their companies on the right path for growth. Before they hired us to get the meetings for them, they couldn't get enough of the right meetings to achieve the growth they wanted. In all those years I have watched many leaders take the opportunity and run with it, putting their companies on the map and experiencing growth that exceeded even their most optimistic goals.

In that same time, I've also observed owners of growing businesses take a few wrong turns, making mistakes that have caused them to unnecessarily waste time and money and ultimately to miss out on important opportunities. Among the thousands of decisions business owners make regarding messaging, planning, hiring, and lead cultivation, it's not always easy to see which is the most direct path to the cash. It's hard to know where you got off track, and it's even harder to ensure it won't happen again.

The good news is that with the right planning, tools, and guidance, you *can* do business development right. You can avoid unnecessary detours and chart the most direct path to market domination (if that's what you want). My co-author, Carl, and I wrote this book because we've biked the business development trail many times with a multitude of clients. We want to help you avoid taking a wrong path leading to too much exertion for too little reward. We want to give you the knowledge and strategies you need to ensure you take the right path the first time so that you achieve the growth and lasting success you want without the unnecessary twists and turns along the way.

CARL HERE!

Caryn and I worked together to develop the content for this book, however, we thought it would be less confusing for our readers if it came to you primarily in her voice. I will be weighing in from time to time with my own stories and anecdotes that relate to a particular point.

For anyone who hasn't read my first book, *The 7 Stages of Small-Business Success*, I am a lifelong entrepreneur as well as a business mentor and coach. After launching and selling my first few businesses, I began working with leaders of small-

and medium-sized ventures to make sure they are structured and equipped for long-term growth. Like Caryn, I've seen a lot of unnecessary detours, but I've also been privileged to ensure all my clients get Biz Dev Done Right!

CHAPTER 1

BUSINESS DEVELOPMENT DONE RIGHT

– Definition.

WHAT IS BUSINESS DEVELOPMENT?

N ext time you're in a room full of business owners, try asking ten of them to define business development. Chances are, you'll get ten different answers. Some might use the term interchangeably with "marketing," while others think of business development as whatever the sales team does all day. A lot of people go to school to learn business development, but you can complete hundreds of hours of coursework without mastering the activities critical to realizing strong sales as quickly as possible. So what *is* business development, really?

Carl and I define business development very simply: new dollars. They could be new dollars from new clients or more dollars from existing clients. Regardless of where they come from, the easiest way to understand business development is the act of bringing in revenue that you've never had before.

In this chapter, you'll get a crystal clear picture of what good business development is and what it is not. You'll learn which activities lead directly to an increase in revenue and which are a lower priority. Most importantly, you'll be able to determine if you are setting your company up for optimal results, and if you're not, you'll be able to correct course.

WHAT BUSINESS DEVELOPMENT IS

Most of us know good business development when we see it. A company doing it right will be growing: increasing its profits and reaching new markets. From the outside it looks like a well-oiled machine, but inside the salespeople are hard at work bringing in those new dollars. When business development is done right, those new dollars will exceed your attrition rate. That means your revenue is actually growing, not just making up for any customers you might lose.

Business Development is the act of bringing in revenue...

...that you've never had before.

Business owners who are able to make this happen don't do it by accident. They have a clearly articulated plan to secure those new dollars, and they take specific, deliberate steps to carry out that plan. Above all, they understand that the heart of business development is building and nurturing the right relationships.

Business Development Is a Clear Path to New Dollars

We will cover business development plans in much more detail in chapter 2, but for now, keep in mind that business development done right is always based on a realistic and clearly defined path to new dollars. Most businesses have at least a small built-in market. Girl Scouts sell cookies to their parents and grandparents. Neighborhood businesses can easily sell to the people who pass by their locations on a daily basis. Real estate agents and financial planners probably have friends and family members as their first clients.

In all these cases, a vital part of business development is expanding beyond the immediate circle of relational and geographical influence. New businesses can have a good base of customers and achieve organic growth. But too often they grow by accident through leveraging their referral networks. Only when they've exhausted those networks do they discover the importance of growing on purpose. This is where many missteps occur and why it's so important to chart that clear path to new dollars ahead of time.

Business Development Is Strategic, Purposeful, and Ongoing

Business development is not a one-time event, nor is it only for new companies. It is a strategic process that is carried out consistently and purposefully for the rest of your company's life, and business owners doing it right are both prepared and persistent.

The Importance of Preparation

Every year on the Fourth of July, Atlanta hosts about 60,000 runners for the Peachtree Road Race. It's a 10K, not a marathon, so people of varying athletic abilities participate. Whether you run or watch, you'll notice a huge difference between the people who have trained for the race and those who haven't. And athletic looks and expensive running shoes don't tell the whole story. In fact, you might even see moms pushing jogging strollers faster than some younger men are running, all because the moms took the time to prepare.

All successful business development begins with purposeful and deliberate preparation. Just like the winner of the Peachtree was training long before race day, the key to turning sales activities into new dollars for your business begins before you ever pick up the phone or sit down at a meeting. This may sound very straightforward, but in my experience, fewer than 20 percent of business owners and salespeople prepare properly for activities like prospect phone calls, meetings, conferences, and networking events.

Simply put, 100 percent of the top performers prepare, while imposters are content to improvise. This is not just true in business; you see it in everything from sports to politics and the performing arts. Olympic gymnasts train thousands of hours for four minutes of competition. Political candidates spend millions of dollars crafting a message for a 30-second television ad. And bands that have been around for decades still rehearse for shows, because they aren't willing to leave anything to chance. Companies that do business development right make it a priority to strategically prepare their personnel for sales opportunities with the same sense of purpose.

In the business world, like everywhere else, imposters can do a very good job disguising themselves as professionals. Just as the race participant who's been sitting on the couch for the last six months can still show up in the best running gear, imposters can dress the part and talk the talk. In fact, many business owners have wasted valuable time and money hiring imposters who looked the part. They may ace the job interview, but when it comes to the sales process they'll neglect preparation, throwing out buzz words and jargon instead of meaningful content. They'll send the same email to a thousand prospects and expect a response. The business owner who mistakenly chooses the imposter for a sales rep has no hope of doing business development right. (We'll cover hiring in detail in chapter 6.)

Professionals, on the other hand, will prepare their sales presentations to the point where they sound natural, not rehearsed. They'll not only be able to connect well with the prospect, but they'll also bring meaningful content to the interaction.

At a networking event, the imposter will walk into a room and talk about himself to anyone who will listen. He'll give and collect as many cards as possible and pat himself on the back afterward for having such a productive day. In contrast, the professional will research beforehand who will be attending the event, and he'll often make contact with key people ahead of time to let them know he is looking forward to meeting them. He will ask the organizers to introduce him to his priority prospects, and he'll be prepared with a meaningful message explaining why meeting with him will make the prospect's life better. He also exchanges cards, but he follows up within 24 hours to solidify the next step in the relationship. Both the imposter and the professional spent the same of amount of time at the event, but only the professional is likely to see new dollars as a result of his efforts.

The Importance of Persistence

We tend to think of high-level executives in large companies as a sort of royalty—aloof and removed from the everyday problems of regular people like us. But in reality, they are human beings, just like you and me. They lose things, forget engagements, run out of time, and get stressed out. And like everyone else in the world, they want to be listened to, appreciated, and cared about.

On a recent plane ride, I happened to sit next to a high-level decision maker at a major electronics company. We got to talking, and I asked her what it was like to be contacted all the time by people hoping to win her as a client. She offered a few thoughts, we chatted about other things, and then she fell asleep. At the very end of the flight when she woke up, she said to me, "You know, I have to tell you: my biggest pet peeve with the people who call me is that if I don't have an immediate need, they blow me off. Six months later, I could totally need what they have, but they're long gone. It's like they pretend to care about me at first, but they drop me if I can't boost their sales right now." She went on to say that she was incredibly offended that they would waste her time and that she would never, ever work with people who did that.

This woman was just like anyone else. She had a tremendous amount of responsibility, and the right vendors could really make her life a lot easier. But because most vendors were only interested in a quick sale instead of building an ongoing relationship with her, they missed out on tremendous opportunities.

A "no" from a prospect may simply mean "I don't need your product or service right now, but I might need it soon." Far too many people assume that the lack of an immediate need or even a mere failure to return a phone call means the potential client isn't interested at all. Others move on because they don't see an opportunity for a quick sale.

Generally speaking, if decision makers can potentially benefit from what you offer, there is no reason to stop contacting them unless you obtain new information that leads you to believe they are no longer good prospects. Otherwise, continue to think up different ways to approach them. Most likely, your competition won't.

Years ago, one of my clients was offering his services to a large pharmaceutical company where one of the high-level decision makers was very attached to her existing vendors. For years, the only answer my client heard was "Thank you, but no thank you." But I kept reminding him to hang in there, because the decision maker was close to retirement age.

So my client kept calling, and one day a male voice answered the phone. The woman had retired, and her replacement was ready to reevaluate everything. Before we knew it, my client was in the door. Some might ask why he was calling one company for years when he was only being told no. But someone doing business development right understands that a short phone call every few months can eventually yield great rewards.

Business Development Is About the Right Relationships

Professionals doing business development right create and nurture relationships that will not only bring new clients but also bring new dollars from existing clients. They identify the right prospects, make the initial connection, and build trust. While following up, they confirm that the prospect is a good fit for the company, and then close sales and grow sales with those new clients.

Cultivating the Right Relationships

Building the right business development relationships requires consistent follow-up, which takes significant time and planning. The price of *not* following up, however, can be huge. I know someone else who spent a few thousand dollars to travel to a trade show, where she met a decision maker, "Jack." They connected well, and he gave her his office number and asked her to call. She made the first call, but the project Jack needed her for had been put on hold. Instead of following up with Jack in a month or two, she figured that he would contact her when he was ready.

The following year, she spent another few thousand dollars to go back to the same trade show where she ran into Jack again. He greeted her warmly and told her that he had been looking for her card. He had gotten cleared to go ahead with the project six months after her initial call, and his company had ended up spending $3 million dollars on it. Unfortunately, because he couldn't find her card, he went with another vendor.

Should you stop following up if a buyer selects another vendor? Even then, I advise my clients to follow up at reasonable intervals. In one case, three companies competed for a three-year multimillion-dollar contract. Of the two companies that were not awarded the contract, one disappeared while the other called the buyer every month. This was a short call: "How's it going? Are you happy? Anything I can do to help you?"

Every month for a year the buyer answered that things were going well. And then something changed. There was a personnel change with the vendor that won the contract, and the buyer was no longer happy. She tried to fix it, but it became clear it wasn't fixable. So she decided to terminate the contract. And instead of going back out to the market with another request for proposal (RFP), she just handed the entire project over to the business owner who had stayed in touch.

Of course there can be good reasons to stop contacting a prospective client. You could obtain new information that indicates a particular company or individual is no longer a good prospect for your business. But until then, stay with it. As author Dan Kennedy says, the only difference between garbage and salad is timing!

CARL'S COMMENTS:

My business trains numerous business-growth consultants, and one of the tools we give them is my first book, *The 7 Stages of Small-Business Success*. Our consultants often give a copy of the book to prospective clients as part of the packet of information that explains what we do. One of our consultants, "Susie," went to a networking meeting and met a new business owner, "Cathy," who was very interested in our services. They had a great conversation, and Susie gave Cathy the information packet and the book.

About a year later, my wife and I went to that same networking meeting and gave her card to a lot of great people. A couple days later, a woman showed up in our office. We sat down with her, and she pulled out copy of *The 7 Stages of Small-Business Success*. It was dog-eared and full of notes in the margins.

"I've been reading this book," she explained, "and I know just what I want to do. I just need an advisor who can take me through the process." Of course my wife and I looked at each other and laughed, explaining to the woman that I was the author of the book.

It turns out, the woman in front of us was Cathy from the networking meeting a year ago. Susie had not followed up with her effectively, so my wife ending up coaching Cathy through the process of growing her business.

The late sales guru Chet Holmes—author of the book *The Ultimate Sales Machine* and a former client of mine—used to tell the story of how he called a prospect for 12 years. That might seem like a long time, but at the end of those 12 years, he entered into a business partnership with Tony Robbins. Sounds like time well spent to me.

Maximizing the Right Relationships

Maximizing the relationships you cultivate means you find ways to get new dollars from existing clients. Generally speaking, you want to work to increase your share of sale with your clients that may need more from you. You want to purposefully work toward getting a bigger "piece of the pie." You also want to think of creative ways to grow the overall pie, if at all possible. One of my clients, "Tom," owned a business that monograms T-shirts and other items, and he was working with a large client company, "ClientCo." ClientCo had almost 100 different decision makers with budgets, and Tom knew one of them. I knew immediately that my job was to help him get in front of the other 99.

The decision maker that Tom had built a relationship with purchased about 50 T-shirts for a charity walk his department was sponsoring. So I asked Tom the key questions: What else? Who else? How can you make this opportunity bigger? What else could we sell this decision maker, and who else might want to buy these T-shirts? After all, ClientCo had 20,000 employees. A sale of 50 T-shirts was just scratching the surface.

Tom thought about the questions; he knew of a second charity walk that the department was sponsoring later in the year, which would more than double the order. We talked some more, and we decided to offer water bottles and key chains in addition to T-shirts. I continued to ask Tom for more possibilities until he was stumped.

Then I asked Tom to think big: "What about the other people in the company who don't get to go on the walk? Would they want to wear a T-shirt in support of the 50 people who do?" Tom offered this option to the decision maker, and he loved it. It just so happened that ClientCo was looking for opportunities to promote interdepartmental cooperation, and the T-shirt offer fit perfectly. This dramatically increased the size of the order and opened the door for Tom to meet with heads of other departments.

In my experience, about nine out of ten business owners and sellers don't think to take these additional steps once they're in the door with a particular client organization. It takes a little more thought and planning: you need to stay alert for openings that might not be obvious. But if you keep asking yourself "What else?" and "Who else?" and "What's bigger than that?" as you continue to cultivate your relationships, you may be surprised how many opportunities you'll uncover. They can triple your business or more!

Business Development Is Executed by the Right People Following the Right Process

A company that wants to succeed will hire sellers with the right level of skill and experience. It helps significantly if they have sales in their DNA. A company that wants to succeed will also have a sound process for sellers to follow, a solid training/onboarding program to show them how to apply selling skills to the process, and management supervision to ensure compliance and goal achievement. What do you do if the sellers you have are not the best sellers for the job? One option is training, another is splitting the job function to leverage individual strengths, and a third is outsourcing the portion(s) of the sales process that isn't being done well. If these options don't work, then consider replacing the sellers (we'll cover this in more detail in chapter 9, "Coach 'Em Up or Coach 'Em Out").

Your sales process has to be so airtight that if you thought you hired an "A" seller but later find out you have a "C," the person can still operate productively until you find a better alternative. The right process can turn a willing amateur into a more polished professional who not only knows what to do but does it consistently. On the other hand, you can have a great product and a great sales team, but without the right process for the sales team to follow, you will fall short in business development.

One component of the right process is executing the right follow-up. There is a consistent forward momentum to business development done right. If too much time goes by between a follow-up request from the decision maker and the response from the seller, the prospect may conclude that the seller doesn't really care about solving his problems. The right process—immediate, consistent follow-up—builds trust and keeps the momentum going. In addition, if a seller doesn't do what she says she will do in the business development time period, how can the decision maker be confident that the seller will do what she promises if she becomes a vendor?

Not all follow-up is created equal. You can follow up diligently and still not get anywhere. What makes the difference between a welcome follow-up call and a nuisance? The answer is extremely simple: bring value to every conversation you have and every connection you make.

We're all busy, so it can be very tempting to make a quick follow-up call and check it off the list. I call this the tick-mark syndrome, since the seller is more gratified by putting a tick-mark next to an item on a task list than by actually getting results. It's far more time consuming to study your prospects' needs and prepare an approach that brings value to the interaction. But the sellers who do this will get significantly better results for time spent than those who just make the quick call.

Unfortunately, some managers unintentionally incentivize the "tick-mark" syndrome. They focus on the number of calls and emails their sales team is completing rather than what is accomplished during each interaction. This rewards quantity rather than quality, which ultimately wastes everyone's time.

Business Development Is Managed by People Who Incentivize Results, Diagnose Problems, and Implement the Correct Solutions

We'll cover management strategies in much greater detail in chapter 9, but for now, here are a few key points to keep in mind. Too often, incentives from managers don't encourage the exact behaviors that lead to desired results, causing those results to fall short of expectations. Managers and owners are often angry that they paid incentives when they didn't achieve what they wanted. They don't realize that the results are disappointing because they are rewarding the wrong behaviors. Managers may be unaware of a problem or may not know how to diagnose where it's coming from. This may cause them to make changes but still experience the same issues six months down the road. In this case it can be helpful to get an opinion from an outside expert. When you correctly identify the problem and fix it the first time, you will implement the correct solution and be on the path to getting business development right.

WHAT BUSINESS DEVELOPMENT IS NOT

Just as there is little to no consensus about what business development *is,* there is tremendous confusion about activities that are often categorized as business development but most certainly are *not.* Carl and I have compiled a list of the major offenders here:

Business Development Is NOT Marketing

Marketing is important, but it is not business development. Billboards, television or radio ads, internet and social media campaigns, and mass email marketing can all be important in your company's plan, but they do not lead directly to new dollars.

Business Development Is NOT Processing Sales You Would Have Anyway

Maintaining a website, swiping credit cards, renewing contracts, answering inbound calls, and taking orders are not business development accomplishments. Those activities merely process sales you already have—the equivalent of operating the cash register at a store; they don't bring in new dollars. Confusion over this difference has a price: many business owners hire people with only transactional sales experience for business development positions. The new hires may have experience processing incoming orders or leads that were handed to them after the heavy lifting on the sale was completed by someone else. Without the right experience or training, they will not be prepared to bring in new dollars.

That said, it's always a good idea to train personnel involved in order processing to upsell or customize orders. Good servers at restaurants will always showcase an appetizer and a dessert; they'll know liquors well enough to offer top shelf options and wine well enough to suggest a selection that complements an entrée choice. Whatever the position, employees can be involved in business development if they go beyond maintaining and processing what you already have.

CARL'S COMMENTS:

Last summer, I got a call from Scott, the guy who runs the ticket agency in my hometown, alerting me that I still needed to pick up Yankees tickets I had purchased. After I made arrangements to pick them up, Scott chimed in, "I noticed that for the past two years you've gone to the U.S. Open. Are you thinking of going again?" I told him I was, and he began asking me what I enjoyed most about the experience. I explained that my wife and I are huge tennis fans and that the Open falls near our anniversary. After we chatted a while, I purchased all-day VIP passes that I never even knew existed. Scott went beyond being an order taker to bringing me value. He not only got a great sale for himself, but he gave my wife and me an unforgettable anniversary.

Business Development Is NOT about You

Business development is about your clients and prospects; it is not about you. This very simple truth is often overlooked by salespeople who are eager to impress, enjoy hearing themselves talk too much, or just need to close some sales. But if you diligently guard against these potential pitfalls, you can keep your sales team's focus in the right place.

Don't Show Off

Business development is about meeting the needs of your prospective clients, not showing off how smart you are or all the technical jargon you learned when you got your latest certification. Unfortunately, many people get in front of a prospect and try to convince him (or her) how much they know. Remember, your prospects care if you can make their lives easier, not if you have 12 postgraduate degrees.

If you find yourself talking most of the time during your prospect meetings, something may be wrong. There can be a fine line between proving you know what you're talking about and focusing on the prospects' issues and challenges. Even if you don't mean to, it's easy to get ahead of yourself, trying to close the sale before the prospect has agreed he or she needs your products or services. Remember, your goal is to find out what your prospects need and communicate clearly how and why you can meet that need better than anyone else (or better than the current solution they have in place). This means you will be listening and asking questions, not just talking.

Don't Write Book-Length Proposals

When it comes to writing proposals or even just emails, less is often more. Your goal is to create proposals that strategically and deliberately lead your prospect to say yes. The best way to do this is to be short and to the point, keeping your language focused on what the prospect has expressed is most important, not adding extraneous unnecessary information. Your prospects want to read something that applies to them and helps them make a decision.

I've helped clients turn 30-page proposals into four pages, by focusing on only the most relevant material and putting secondary but important information into an appendix. These kinds of editing decisions help keep any written communication with your prospect straightforward, as well as easy to read and understand.

Remember, you want your written communication to put people in a "yes" mode, not a "maybe" mode. A proposal that's too long or complicated often gets put to the side to be reviewed "later." But sometimes later never comes, and the prospect will decide on a vendor whose proposal was short, easy to understand, and answered his needs. Make it easy for your prospects to read your proposal and say yes, or you'll be pushing them toward your competitors.

CARL'S COMMENTS:

Not long ago, I called our remote IT tech about an urgent matter in our office. He lives two hours away, but I was ready to pay him well to come handle our issue in person. Meaning well, he kept explaining to me that this would mean four hours in the car for him to do about thirty minutes of work and that there were local resources that could handle our problem cheaper. I kept trying to interrupt him to explain that money really wasn't the issue in this situation, but he continued to try to educate me against my will about the details of his job.

If he'd been a little more tuned into my needs, he could have made more of his trip by saying something like, "Well, as long as I'm coming by, do you need any of your other machines looked at?" But instead he kept telling me information I didn't need. You want to bring value to your clients and act in their best interests, but when you have a sale, close it and be done!

Business Development Is NOT a Few Calls on a Friday Afternoon Because You Have Extra Time

Have you ever purchased a fresh baguette from a bakery? Crispy on the outside and soft on the inside, the tantalizing aroma makes you want to cut into it right away. But what will happen if you savor that first piece with some butter and then forget about the rest of it for a couple of days? Of course it will go stale and the loaf will be completely wasted.

Too often, busy entrepreneurs and sellers try to squeeze in business development in their spare time, initiating relationships and then letting them go stale. Business development just isn't something you can stop when something else comes up and then start again when you have a spare moment. Random or spontaneous sales activities not only fail to produce the desired results, but they are also impossible to evaluate effectively.

Once you have that clear path to new dollars, it takes disciplined leadership to ensure that sellers understand the plan and follow it consistently. Consistent, deliberate business development allows you to evaluate your processes and tweak them as needed. In the next chapter, Carl and I will give you the keys to writing a business development plan that will allow you to get the results you want while constantly improving how you do it.

CHAPTER 2

THE MISSING LINK IN YOUR BUSINESS DEVELOPMENT

– What's Missing?

THE MISSING LINK IN YOUR BIZ DEV PLAN

A business development plan is a plan of action. It is a written document that explains the goals of your business and how you are going to achieve them. It contains background information such as market research and analysis, but more importantly, it contains the detailed steps you will take to bring new dollars to your company.

This chapter will give you an overview of the business development process itself, as well as specific steps for converting leads into appointments. It will also offer key insight into the most common omissions in the planning process to help you uncover any missing links in your own business development plan.

RIGHT ACTIONS AND ACTIVITIES

Every great edifice, from the Taj Mahal to the Eiffel Tower, began as a set of plans. And just as builders work from blueprints, your sellers need a detailed step-by-step plan to guide their daily activities.

A well-conceived plan allows you to be deliberate and methodical in your business development; it also allows you to evaluate each step of the process and make adjustments when necessary. But in reality, many new businesses get going without any such plan in place. Entrepreneurs start with an idea for a product or service, make that idea a reality, and then take whatever business comes their way. If you ask them how they get new dollars through the door, they may give you a blank look or a vague answer: "Oh, we network, sign a contract, and get paid in 90 days."

These kinds of business owners tend to think of business development very imprecisely: just getting more leads or more customers somehow. They can actually get by this way for a while, but ultimately if they don't fill in the significant gaps in their "plan," they're going to miss out on optimal growth and risk losing market share to the competition.

A sound business development plan gives your sellers a road map to success. Henry Ford's Model T assembly line revolutionized the auto industry by breaking down the creation of an automobile into thousands of simple, repeatable steps. Not one person in his factory could have put an entire car together by himself, but everyone could do his job quickly and well. In the same way, a sound business development plan lays out a clear path to closed sales for any willing seller by breaking the sale down into bite-sized, repeatable steps.

Furthermore, the right plan will not just make your sales goals possible, it will also make them inevitable. Let's suppose your salespeople typically close about one in ten of their appointments, and your current company goal is to have one new deal a month. Going out on ten appointments with qualified leads makes closing one deal a realistic expectation. But if your salesperson went out on 30 appointments in a month, one deal should be inevitable. After all, any salesperson who can't close 1 in 30 qualified leads should probably look for a different job.

The better your plan, the more your goals will not be dependent on factors you cannot control, such as market fluctuations or other economic environmental factors. Of course, your plan will also have to address the fact that you can't simply decide to go out on 30 appointments a month; you have to determine in detail how you are going to obtain 30 appointments. How many can you reasonably expect from search engine optimization (SEO), from networking, and from your other outbound lead generation efforts? The right business development plan incorporates these realistic estimates and then focuses on how many calls you make and how you build the list of people you're going to call in the first place. These are all within your control, and once you make those 30 appointments a month inevitable, your goal of one new deal a month is also inevitable.

WHAT IS YOUR MAGIC BULLET?

CARL'S COMMENTS:

Several years ago, a client of mine, "Rick," was invited to speak on a panel to explain how he had been able to grow his business so effectively when his entire industry was struggling. He asked me to join him, and since the event was local and Rick and I needed to talk anyway, I agreed.

Rick spoke, and as you might expect, he started getting peppered with questions about how he was developing his business so well in such a challenging economy. "So what's your magic bullet?" a guy in the front row inquired.

I had just bitten into a cookie when Rick responded, "Well, my advisor is here. Why don't we bring him up to answer that?" So I swallowed my food and pulled out a folded piece of paper—my notes for my later meeting with Rick—on which

I had written a Nine-Step Overview of the Business Development Process. You could have heard a pin drop in the room as I spoke, and I was bombarded by questioners afterward. (Come to think of it, I don't think I ever got to finish that cookie!)

Here are the nine steps Carl shared with the people in the room that night and with countless clients since:

1. **Strategic Planning.** Outline what you're selling to whom. Write down how much you hope to sell and how you're going to get as close as possible to 100 percent share of sale. This step includes outlining strategies for branding and marketing, detailing the profile of your ideal client, and setting goals and benchmarks for sales.

2. **Marketing.** For our purposes in this book, the practical application of marketing is to generate qualified leads. Start marketing based on your plan. We advise clients to have a minimum of five proactive, lead-generating campaigns running at all times. These will include networking, outbound marketing, internet, and social media.

3. **Leads.** Branding and public relations are important, but if your marketing is not generating qualified leads, it's not working. You could pay a few million dollars for a Super Bowl ad and get your company recognized across the country. You could have millions of followers on Twitter and Instagram. But if those activities don't lead to you getting more interactions with the right kind of

prospects, then you're most likely wasting your time and money.

4. **Conversation.** This is the initial conversation with the prospect where you discuss the prospects' needs and interests, based on what you have to offer.

5. **Qualification.** Everyone understands the qualification process when it comes to buying a car or a house: either buyers pay with cash or they get approved for the right kind of loan. But almost every economic transaction has some sort of qualification process to it. Restaurant and retail customers also have to be able to afford their purchases by bringing the right amount of cash or having room on their credit cards.

But affordability isn't the only factor when it comes to qualification. After the release of the most recent Camaro SS, a Chevy dealer was about to sell one to a customer for cash. Normally this wouldn't be an issue, but the buyer was 104 years old. The dealer understandably wasn't completely sure about selling him a 427 horsepower vehicle. So the dealer took the buyer out for a test drive. The customer proved to be about as fit as you could be at any age, so they closed the deal.

6. **Transaction**. This step clearly defines the transaction that is about to take place. At the movies, for example, the cashier will confirm the number of tickets you want for

which showing and confirm whether you are paying with a credit card or cash.

7. **Paperwork**. This step formalizes the transaction you have just defined. It can be as complicated as the stacks of papers a buyer has to sign to purchase a house or as simple as presenting a check at a restaurant and getting the credit card slip signed.

8. **Approval**. You might think once the paperwork is complete that all is well, but often there is still an approval process to complete. Sometimes a manager or a superior needs to sign off on the transaction. Other times, certain laws or regulations apply to the sale. Just because two parties agree to an exchange and spell it out in terms they both like doesn't mean the transaction is legal or finished.

CARL'S COMMENTS

I once bought a lake that could have landed me in jail. The colleague who owned the park containing the lake felt bullied by the state of New Jersey, which at the time was busy acquiring green space for protection. So he wanted to sell the property to anyone but the state, and I was on hand with the money.

We agreed to terms we were both comfortable with and drew up a deed of sale. I showed it to my lawyer, excited for him to see what a good deal I was getting. I was a little taken aback when he responded, "So which jail should I plan to bail you out of?" He explained that our agreement, although we both were pleased with it, violated four different state and local laws. Needless to say we made a few modifications, closed the sale, and no one went to prison!

9. **Close.** The close, of course, is when money actually changes hands and your clients receive the goods or services they paid for.

These nine steps might seem extremely detailed, but if any one of them goes wrong, you could lose the sale. More involved activities like strategic planning or marketing take a lot more time than running a credit card, but if your credit card machine gets compromised, you are in big trouble. Sound business development plans pay attention to all the little details so that nothing big or small will hinder you from reaching both your short-term and long-term goals. For a Biz Dev Done Right planning template, go to www.BizDev-DoneRightBook.com/BizDevPlanningTemplate.com

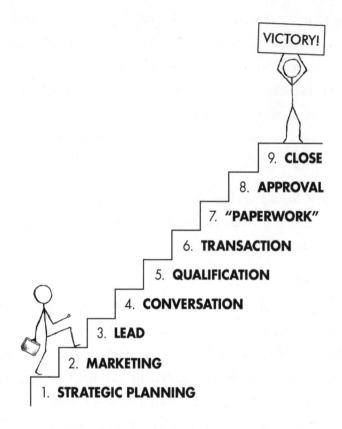

THE PATH TO THE CASH!®

The path between step 3 (leads) and step 4 (conversations) of the business development process can be mired with difficulty for many business owners. Many of my clients tell me, "If I could just get in front of the right prospect, I know I could close the sale. I just can't get in front of enough of the right prospects." I'm often asked to diagnose why companies are not getting more meetings for the time they're spending prospecting. So what does it take to convert your leads into actual conversations with your prospects?

Imagine your ideal clients are on the other side of a door locked with a combination lock. You could start trying random combinations to see if you get lucky, or you could try a hacksaw or an ax to get in by force. But of course the easiest way would be to learn the combination that will open the lock. When companies are not converting enough leads into conversations, I look for problems in five major areas. When each of these areas is working well, the doors will open.

1. Target

The first "number" in the combination is to choose the right target. Many companies waste a lot of time on prospects they shouldn't be targeting. Sometimes business owners haven't taken the time to define carefully who belongs on their list. In other cases they defined the ideal client a couple of years ago, but no one has been checking up on the salespeople to see if they're still pursuing the right group of prospects. In other cases, the originally identified group was right at the time, but when market conditions changed, the target group should have changed as well. Good prospects are not solely defined by the amount of money they have but by how quickly and readily they will buy from you. Good prospects are also far more likely to buy from you multiple times and refer their friends, colleagues, and family members to do the same.

You could be the best salesperson in the world, but you will get nowhere if you're targeting the wrong group of people. You want to make sure you are investing your time and energy into the individuals and companies that can truly benefit from what you have to offer. They will say yes much faster and more often than the general population, and they will lead you to the referrals and repeat business you want. You will get better results from ten hours spent pursuing members of the right target group than from 100 hours spent pursuing the masses.

2. Sales Message

Sales messaging is different from branding and marketing messages. There could be two equally accurate ways to describe your product or service; one will resonate with prospects while the other will leave them cold. And since it takes the same amount of time to market an effective message as it does an ineffective one, you might as well go with the one that achieves results. To do this you need to craft the language that will cause your prospects' eyes to light up, not glaze over. This includes compelling talking points for both voicemail and live conversation, whether the prospect comes from inbound or outbound activity. (We'll cover messaging a lot more in chapter 4.)

3. Objection Answers

I've trained a lot of salespeople over the years, and the majority of them ad lib their answers to a typical objection instead of going into the selling situation prepared. When you get just one opportunity to speak with a prospect, it's critical to make the most of it. You don't typically get a second chance to get it right.

Trial lawyers wouldn't dream of entering the courtroom unprepared. They think of every possible angle, any possible objection the other attorney will have, issues witnesses will raise, and so on, so that no matter how the conversation goes, they always remain in control. In the movie *A Few Good Men* we saw Tom Cruise and Demi Moore spend hours preparing for every possible scenario. They researched, interviewed people, and created compelling reports so that Tom could expertly lead the discussion to his intended outcome. It doesn't mean that there weren't a few surprises for him. There were. But he was well equipped to handle them thanks to the preparation he put in before he was in front of the people he needed to convince.

Likewise, comedians take the stage knowing they will face hecklers, just as speakers expect to encounter skeptics when they deliver a speech. Both prepare their performances with these people in mind.

Not long ago, my company was hired to get a client meetings with vice presidents of large banks. One of my team members was in the process of door opening, when one of the vice presidents presented a very strong objection to taking the meeting with our client. But our Door Opener® had a very strong, one-sentence answer for the objection. When the vice president heard it, he paused and said, "Huh. I hadn't thought about it like that. I do need to have that meeting." And they set the date and time.

My client met with the vice president and closed a deal worth $805,000 *annually.* All because of a one-sentence answer to an objection. If our seller hadn't had that answer, there wouldn't have been an $805,000 sale. The fact that our Door Opener® knew the right answer that flipped the prospect's "no" to a "yes, it's important we meet" was no accident. We had carefully crafted the answers to the objections we expected before the program went live. Our Door Opener® was completely prepared when he received the objection, and the results prove it.

Unfortunately, I've seen far too many salespeople sweat, stammer, and completely lose control of a prospect conversation because they weren't prepared to answer an objection. Situations like this are the reason my company has developed an entire manual devoted to answering objections that keep sellers from getting in the door with prospects. It offers a variety of answer options that can be utilized based on how the prospect is posing the objection. One answer for a particular objection might be in the form of a question that will get the prospect talking more. Another answer for the same objection might be a success story. A third option might be a visual image, a graph or picture that the salesperson can have handy if it's needed.

Well-prepared sellers pre-think potential objections before they enter selling situations and know the answers. They remain in control of the discussion.

I highly recommend sales managers have their sellers demonstrate proficiency in answering challenging objections before their sellers are unleashed on the company's most important prospects. (We'll discuss the demonstration of proficiency more in chapter 8.)

Remember, the objection is not an insult to you or your company. It is actually a necessary part of the sales process, and it is evidence that the prospect is truly engaged. The answer to the objection is so crucial that it should not be left to chance. Remember, if you can't overcome an objection, you will never close the sale.

Ultimately, it is the business owner's responsibility to make sure that the sellers are prepared with the right answers. Monitor the selling process, and if you find sellers are getting challenged by a particular objection you didn't anticipate, work with them to develop a better answer and watch your sales increase. Every company should have an objections manual, a living document that includes the best, most effective answers for challenging objections at every phase of the sales process. Most companies don't have this, but those who do win.

One of my company's clients has three sellers. Two of them complained to me that every time they faced a particular objection, they lost the sale. I was having breakfast in Chicago with the third seller and told her about the troubles the other two were having. She said, "That objection? That one is easy." She proceeded to share a brilliant answer that worked for her every time. The problem was that the other two sellers didn't know she had the right answer. Two-thirds of the times the company faced that objection they lost the sale. Ouch. It would not have been that way if there had been a central place where company objection answers were stored and the sellers had been required to know the answers and demonstrate proficiency in using the answers in the right situations.

4. Seller

High-level decision makers are busy, and as I've said, you often get only one shot with them. The sales skills it takes to get the meetings are not necessarily the same skills it takes to do a good job in the meetings and in closing the sales. With the example of the bank vice president, our Door Opener® succeeded because he was exceptionally experienced and intuitive and wanted to do the job of door opening. How far would he have gotten with the vice president if he hadn't had the skills, experience, or desire?

Years ago a client hired my company to develop their outbound sales messaging, but they selected a different company to make the calls to get the meetings. The client was very happy with the messaging we crafted, but the calls the other company was making for him weren't generating much business. I offered to listen to the calls to see if I could discern the problem, and on one of the first recordings I got, I heard a young girl speaking to a CEO. I was immediately impressed that someone so young was able to get the CEO on the phone. She delivered the messaging that we had written in a nice conversational tone. But then the CEO gave a very fair objection, and instead of giving a productive, confident answer, she giggled. A second later, he hung up.

A good door opener must be able to do more than just call a list of people to get the job done. Productive door opening requires someone who can comfortably and effectively engage decision makers and who understands the nuances involved with persuading busy executives to do something. Add to that the fact that these door-opening conversations often happen in less than 30 seconds and you typically only get one shot, and you'll see why it is critical to have the right seller doing this work for you.

Most business owners know the difference between hunters and farmers. The farmers grow the business, and the hunters close the business. What is in most business owners' blind spot is that within the world of hunters there are those who are great "closers" and others who are great "openers." It's rare to find sellers who are both great openers and great closers. While good hunters are hard to find, it is easier to find a hunter who is great at going on meetings and closing the sale (closer) than the hunter who is crackerjack at initiating new relationships with prospects and getting meetings that others can't get (opener). If you interview for a closer but really need an opener, you are likely to come up short on your sales goals. It's critical to know that not all sellers bring the same set of skills to the table.

In my experience, however, if you pair a great opener with a great closer you'll not only increase your efficiency and success but also see magic happen!

5. Process

The right process ensures that your time, energy, and other resources are being allocated in the right way. Are your door openers spending the right amount of time each week on their tasks? Too many times sellers are burdened (often by management) with non-revenue-generating activities. Remember, if your sellers are spending their time on non-revenue-generating activities, they are *not generating revenue*. Are they making contact with the right reach and frequency so that they're building up a critical mass of relationships? You don't want two months to pass between calls, but you don't want to call every day either. So you want to develop the right process that balances reach and frequency with effective activity. This is what is needed to develop enough of the right relationships to bring enough of the right people to the table for the initial conversations or meetings.

TAKE THE PRESSURE OFF THE CLOSE

Ultimately, a closed sale is really just a simple executional detail of business development well done. When you have all these steps in place and you've provided so much value to the prospect with each one, the closing itself is actually quite simple. It's a logical next step of business development done right.

CARL'S COMMENTS:

In the early days of baseball, it was common for a single pitcher to pitch an entire game. Now pitching staffs are extremely specialized: there's a starting pitcher, a middle relief pitcher, a setup man, and a closer. The New York Yankees had a guy by the name of Mariano Rivera who pitched his last season in 2013. Rivera is regarded as the best closer in the history of baseball. Early in his career, he wasn't particularly impressive as a starting pitcher. He even spent a brief and forgettable period as a shortstop. But then they made him a closer, and he was brilliant. Help all your employees find the niche where they can perform at the highest possible level.

THE MISSING LINK IN BIZ DEV PLANS

As we've already discussed, one of the biggest advantages to spelling everything out in a detailed business development plan is that you can much more effectively determine what is working and what is not. If you're not getting the results you want or expect, the problem could be with just one of your steps. If you're keeping tabs on everything, you'll be able to pinpoint the weak link and make the appropriate adjustments, rather than throwing everything out and starting over. Here are some crucial elements of business development planning that many owners may overlook or neglect:

Identify All Outcomes. You want to clearly and carefully identify all the outcomes you're hoping to achieve. This includes not only the quantitative objectives that can be easily measured but also the incremental steps that will make those numbers a reality. For example, suppose you want to increase your sales by a certain percentage and obtain a certain gross margin. How many new customers will you need to make that happen? What target groups will you draw those customers from? How does your marketing reach those people? Outcomes from each of these smaller steps lead to achieving your stated goals.

Be Realistic. Just because you really want to increase your sales by $3 million doesn't mean that is a realistic goal for you this year. Your goals need to take into account the size and abilities of your sales staff, realistic market conditions, and your organization's capacity to onboard and handle new clients without loss of quality.

Make It Actionable. Builders work from blueprints, not paintings. Just as each line on a blueprint corresponds to the specific placement of a brick or two-by-four, each step in your business development plan outlines an action for your sales staff to complete.

A closed sale is a simple executional detail...

...of business development well done.

Break It Down into Bite-Sized Pieces. A good business development plan breaks the process down into bite-sized pieces and offers realistic estimates of what results to expect at the appropriate time intervals.

Master Each Bite-Sized Piece. It is much less intimidating for the sales staff to master the business development process one step at a time. Whether it's outbound prospect calls, answering inbound requests, initial prospect meetings, follow-up emails, or closing, take the time to train sellers to do each step well.

Take Your Best Guess. With so many steps to plan, how do you know when you're ready to move forward with implementation? Once you grasp the subtle details that are vital to business development done right, it's easy to become hesitant about moving forward out of fear of getting something wrong.

Business is filled with all kinds of factors you can't control. More calculating entrepreneurs, trying to account for every imaginable scenario in their plans, may find this paralyzing. Take your best guess and go for it. Then analyze and tweak your process. Remember to evaluate based on the big picture and many data points over time, not on your worst day.

MONITORING YOUR PLAN: WHAT IS THE RIGHT FREQUENCY?

All parents want to keep an eye on how their children are doing in school. Most of us like to see grades and homework daily, although if life gets crazy we might only check those backpacks two or three times a week. Many school districts even allow parents to sign up for email alerts that notify them when their child's grade changes in a class, making it easy to monitor their progress.

But what if the only news you ever got of your children's performance in school was when you got their quarterly report cards or even their year-end grades? First, it would be too late to do anything about it. Second, it would be very challenging to pinpoint exactly what went wrong and when, because you would be trying to analyze weeks of work all at once.

The same is true of your business development plan. You want to constantly evaluate using realistic criteria so that you can tweak the process when necessary without abandoning an effective overall strategy. If you're not getting enough meetings, is it the list, the objection answers, the seller who is doing the door opening, the process, or the message? Don't throw them all away before you've figured out the answer.

The best part of regular, systematic monitoring is that you also get to catch your team getting it right! This allows you to reinforce with positive feedback all the actions and activities you want to see and builds momentum toward your goals.

THE PROCESS PICKS UP WHERE THE PERSON DROPS OFF

Remember, the reason Henry Ford didn't have to hire hundreds of automobile engineering geniuses is that he perfected the *process* of putting a Model T together. In the same way, not every seller you hire is going to be a sales strategist, but the right sales process will enable any willing seller to be more successful.

In fact, I've found that sometimes sellers may have been successful at a previous job due to a sound process more than an extraordinary skill set. When they move to a new company where the process isn't well defined or they don't understand it well, they struggle. That's all the more reason to make sure that your sales process is well thought out so that your sellers don't have to waste time trying to invent it on their own.

KNOW THE TALENT OF YOUR TEAM

It's also important to be realistic about the talent and abilities of your team members so that you can plan based on what they bring to the table. Some will pick up on everything right away, while others will need the steps laid out for them in more detail. It's fine to challenge your team, but don't make the success of your plan contingent on tasks that are realistically beyond their current capabilities. Effective training and monitoring will help you catch issues early so that you can rectify problems and keep your effort on track.

Depending on the size of your company, you may have one employee working on several steps or multiple employees working on the same step. Either way, insert people into the process where they can do their jobs well. This also provides the best opportunities for your employees to grow with your company.

Even if you are running a small or micro business, you probably don't want to handle every single step in-house. You may have strategic partners or alliances, and you always have the ability to outsource any of the steps in the process. Even the smallest of small businesses can effectively compensate for an area of the business development process that they haven't mastered yet through outsourcing.

Good planning will help you identify the areas where you may not have the internal resources to do the best job. My company has helped so many great businesses that have great sellers but just need a little help getting in front of the right prospects. We don't do the entire sales process for them, just the part of the process they are struggling to do well.

BEAT THE COMPETITION...NOW!

The best news is that most of your competition is not taking this level of care with their business development planning. If you do take the time on the front end to plan each step carefully, as well as train and monitor your sales staff effectively, you have a decided competitive advantage.

By now you should be able to identify any missing links in your business development plan. Charles Kettering, the well-known inventor for GM, said, "A problem well stated is a problem half-solved." Developing a detailed and actionable business development plan with realistic targets and a well-thought-out process will put you on the path to creating new dollars. Increased sales will be inevitable.

CHAPTER 3

SALES CYCLE-ONOMICS

– Understanding Your Sales Cycle.

SALES CYCLE-ONOMICS

S ales take time to close. Whether you're launching a new business or growing an established one, the ideal time for a closed sale is usually "yesterday." But we all know that's not how life works. There is a tremendous benefit, however, in being able to predict how long it actually takes you to close a sale from the moment you interact with a new prospect. This chapter will teach you how to calculate that time, how to shorten it, and most of all how to align your selling process with your prospect's buying process. Even though your sales may never close quite as quickly as you'd like, you'll learn how to find your shortest path to the cash!

DEFINING THE SALES CYCLE

Your sales cycle, quite simply, is the length of time from your first interaction with a client to the point at which you have money in hand. For a retail store, this could be a matter of minutes: a new customer enters the store, finds an item, and purchases it. For a business-to-business (B2B) transaction, the process could take several months or even longer.

The sales cycle may begin with a cold call, a networking meeting, a response to an inbound inquiry, or any other initial contact with a lead. It will then typically progress through follow-up phone calls and emails, proposal submissions, and other various meetings. (If the sale comes as a result of an RFP, you may be able to wallpaper your house with the paperwork you'll complete and submit!) After the relationship becomes solid and the client has said yes, the sales cycle finishes when any necessary approvals are complete, the contract is finally signed, and you receive your first payment.

Find the shortest path...

...to the cash!

Understanding your sales cycle is absolutely essential to realistic planning and priority setting for your business. Unfortunately, most business owners engage in wishful thinking when it comes time to define exactly how long it will take for their leads to close. They plan for what they *want* their sales cycle to be rather than for what it actually is. Just like you can't budget based on your best month of revenue if all the other months typically fall much shorter, you can't define your sales cycle based on the quickest sale you ever made.

Besides the nature of your industry itself, three major factors affect the length of your sales cycle:

1. Size of the Sale

Generally speaking, the larger the sale, the longer the sales cycle will be. This is mostly due to the length of the decision-making process and the number of people who will need to approve the transaction. Just like an individual will put more thought into the purchase of a car than a calculator, a company will take longer to sign on the dotted line when there is more money involved.

2. Complexity of the Sale

The second factor affecting the length of your sales cycle is the nature of what you are selling. Are you offering people an item they have already decided to buy or a new service that they're not sure they need? Are you selling your clients a new product or service or replacing (or upgrading) something they already have? Customers buying their first home need a lot more education about the entire process than people who are buying for the second or third time. When you are selling a company something they've never bought before, it is going to take longer to close the sale than if you were simply convincing them to buy from you to replace an existing product or service.

3. Approval Process

Every company has an approval process for purchases, even if it just involves the accounting department signing off on a purchase order. If you're submitting a simple proposal and you're in the door with the one and only decision maker, the sales cycle will be much shorter than if it's an RFP, where multiple proposals will be reviewed by people on a committee. I have led clients through RFPs where they met with each of the decision makers in the approval process before the RFP came out. That way they knew exactly what each committee member was looking for in a vendor relationship. This was an incredibly time-consuming process but worth it! Having insight from each decision maker as to what he or she was looking for was exceptionally helpful for crafting the proposal and navigating the approval process successfully.

In reality, many sellers would love to meet with prospects to find out what they want prior to writing the RFPs, but decision makers will not always agree to do so. Other times, decision makers would be happy to meet, but the sellers didn't think to ask. **Our recommended best practice is that as soon as you receive a request for a proposal or a formal RFP, ask for a date and time to meet (either by phone or in person). This gives you the opportunity to ask key questions that will help you craft the RFP to be nothing short of nirvana for the decision maker.**

Questions to ask in this stage include:

- What is important to you when making a decision about [the product or service]?
- What is important to your boss (or to others on the committee)?
- If all the proposals look the same to you, how will you go about making a decision?
- If all the proposals look different to you, how will you go about making a decision?
- If the proposal looks great to you, what is the approval process in your company? (The answer to this question will not only provide you with the road map to the close, but it will also identify other decision makers who need to be part of the process. This information will help reduce the number of stalled and derailed sales.)
- When do you want the work to start? (You can leverage this information later in the sales process to create urgency if the sale stalls.)

In addition to the type of proposal and approval process, you want to take into account the number of decision makers involved. Obviously a single decision maker will lead to a shorter sales cycle than if you have to submit to a committee. Sometimes more than one department is involved and you need to get each one on board before the process can move forward. All these factors affect your sales cycle, and understanding them can help you plan appropriately. For tips on how to keep your business proposals from the "Big Black Hole," go to www.BizDevDoneRightBook.com/keepingproposals-fromthebigblackhole.com

The Early Bird Gets the Relationship

It is also important to be able to evaluate which stage of the decision-making process your prospective clients are in. Have they already decided they need what you are offering, or are you still trying to educate them about how you can help? It's important to get to them early, but keep in mind that the earlier they are in the decision-making process, the longer it will take to close.

Do not let a longer sales cycle discourage you, however. My door-opening service is often asked to find decision makers who have already concluded they need whatever my client is selling, so we get them in front of those prospects. But in many industries if you reach out to a decision maker who is already in this stage, you're too late: the prospect is already getting ready to close with another vendor, or there is simply not enough time to develop trust before the final decision is made. It's important to get involved with a prospect earlier and give yourself time to develop the relationship. That way you will be part of the decision set when the prospect is ready to go.

If you're the one who educates the prospects about their needs, they are much more likely to buy from you when they are ready to move forward. Even in a case where a certain number of bids are mandated by company policy, getting there early lays the foundation for the relationship. If you've built the relationship early on, you are in a much better position to close the sale.

Ultimately, you win deals when you align your selling process with your client's buying process. It's not about you and when you need the sale; it's about the client's needs and when he or she is ready to buy. This sometimes involves a longer sales cycle, which you have to accept and plan for. And while there's no such thing as being too early to close a sale, you can definitely be too late!

REALITY CHECK

So how do you calculate your real sales cycle? After all, every deal will progress at a different pace. Some deals seem to move forward almost miraculously, while others can drag on forever. We all wish every deal could be like the former, while the latter gives us nightmares. So how do you resist the temptation to take the easiest sale you ever made and calibrate all your expectations against that timeline?

The simplest way to determine your actual sales cycle is to look at your sales over a specific period of time. The length of that time period will vary from industry to industry. For some companies, it may make sense to look at sales over the course of six months; others may need to examine them over two years. Then take out the fastest 10 percent and the slowest 10 percent. The average time it took for the middle 80 percent of your sales to close is the best number to use when predicting your sales cycle. It may not be a number you like, but it's reality, which is where we all need to start.

Your "A" List

Once you have your real sales cycle, start prioritizing your clients. Your A-list clients fit your ideal client profile: they have the resources to buy from you often, and they are likely to refer you to others. They may take longer to close, but if they're good clients they'll be profitable in the long run and aligned with what you want to accomplish. A-level clients buy the right amount at the right price in the right time frame and refer you frequently.

However, there are other clients you'll need to pay attention to as well. Particularly early in your business, it can be challenging to choose between closing sales quickly versus taking the time to cultivate ideal clients. For example, the owners of a graphic design business may want to cultivate leads with large corporations that will spend a lot of money and give their company a great deal of exposure. But these kinds of deals will take a long time to close. In the meantime, they may need to do some smaller contracts for smaller companies or individuals that close in a shorter time frame.

Designing the brochure for a play at a tiny local theater might not be their ideal job, but they may need a few jobs like this to keep the company afloat while they cultivate the longer-term projects. This is a strategic decision to keep the company in a good cash flow position. When planning for their sales cycle, they need to account for the time it will take an ideal client to close, as well as the smaller projects they'll take at the beginning. Carl and I recommend that business owners in these situations devote a set percentage of business development time to pursuing ideal clients.

THE NEW PARADIGM OF SELLING

We can't control the economic climate we work in, but we can face it and make the most of it. Depending on your industry, you could be affected by national and international trends as well as more localized economic realities. In my experience, a slower economy generally results in an elongation of the sales cycle, especially in B2B transactions.

Ten years ago, you could offer to save a company 10 percent on a product or service, and that might have been enough to close the sale. Now, that kind of savings is not worth the time and risk involved for decision makers to upset the status quo. For decision makers to be motivated to act, the change has to benefit them personally in a big way. With this new reality, decision makers are more hesitant to buy, and there are layers of complexity in the approval process that didn't exist before. This means closing a sale takes longer and demands that you nurture leads in a way that actually deepens relationships with decision makers, especially early on.

The kind of nurturing needed in these cases isn't primarily the kind done on the golf course, although there's nothing wrong with that. You cultivate your leads by sharing information of value. This leads your prospects from the stage where they are open to speaking with you about how what you sell can help them, to where they are convinced that they need it ... and you. It may take three interactions or it may take fourteen to move them from the "open stage" to the "convinced stage," so you'll need to gauge where they are and tailor your communications accordingly. Prepare yourself for the marathon and the sprint. A well-thought-out nurture campaign will ensure you have a well-prepared interaction plan that can trigger an earlier close. (Important note: a nurture campaign comprised of periodic noncustomized emails or short emails that say, "Just checking in to see if you have any needs" falls far short of what we call "productive activity." To truly move a relationship forward, customized communication by email and voice must be included.)

In the new paradigm of selling, decision makers don't have time to evaluate another solution without a good reason, so you want each of these communications to demonstrate value for them, which can be the ROI for your product or service. This can include educational material, thought pieces, or explanations of how the work you do is benefiting your existing clientele. This material is much stronger when it includes real numbers or stories which demonstrate that what's in it for them is tangible, not vague or unquantifiable. When putting together your communications, think about your decision makers and how they can justify buying from you to their boss. With these materials, do your best to answer their questions before they ask.

Sometimes the elongation of the sales cycle leads to fatigue on the part of sellers. It can be very tempting to want to skip the steps needed to convince the prospect or build the trust relationship when it feels like the process is taking forever. It can even be tempting to give up entirely. But once you've started the business development process, do not abandon it unless you are convinced that the prospect would no longer make a good client. Too often a seller works hard to get the ball rolling and gives up, only for the competition to step in and close a deal.

Longer sales cycles can be exhausting, but they are the reality we have to deal with when prospective clients are feeling tentative with their dollars. They are often concerned about risking their careers by making the wrong vendor choices or by the amount of time it will take them to implement a different solution. As you plow through the process, remember that those dollars will only be awarded to the vendors with the patience and discipline to see it through to the end.

REASONS TO SAY YES

Given the reality of selling in a challenging economic environment, good business development will involve keeping the process simple while giving the prospect multiple reasons to say yes. In addition to giving all the reasons your product or service is of more value to the decision maker than what your competitors offer or compared with their current solution, it's useful to think in terms of reducing the "friction" or resistance to the transaction itself.

Transactional friction slows down the sales cycle, and it often comes from any risk that may be associated with buying from you. For example, your prospect may be concerned about getting in trouble for choosing you if something goes wrong. Instead of trying to hide or disguise any possible downside of buying from your company, openly acknowledge the potential challenge and explain how you can mitigate any possible problems. For example, if you are located farther away from the prospect than your competitors, explain how that is not an obstacle, as you visit their city frequently already. And just like answering objections and questions, you want to anticipate these causes of "friction" before your prospect brings them up.

FILLING THE EMPTY PIPELINE

Have you ever watched a little boy holding a garden hose while his parent goes to the tap to turn it on? Often, he'll peer into the opening looking impatiently for the water, only to be sprayed in the face when it finally arrives. Just like it takes a while for the water to travel through the garden hose, filling an empty sales pipeline takes time. The point is, if your pipeline is currently empty, don't expect it to fill up immediately if you are just starting new business development efforts. It takes time to fill a pipeline.

When you first launched your business, you may have "force fed" your sales pipeline with shorter sales cycle jobs. (We'll cover the pipeline in much more detail in chapter 5.) These are jobs—like the graphic design company's brochure for the local theater—that you might not take on now that your pipeline is more established. In addition to zeroing in on that ideal client, you may have had to focus on volume. That doesn't mean you accepted everyone who came along, but you may have taken clients who were a degree or two separated from the ideal client. Your hope was they could become that ideal client or they could refer you to ideal clients.

So in those early days, you may have attended events even though the majority of the participants didn't totally fit your ideal client profile. But that process probably helped fill your pipeline and also taught you how to connect with your ideal clients. During this stage it might have felt like you were only adding a few new leads and nurturing some existing leads each month. But all those efforts pushed water into the garden hose. Over time, you developed a more consistent influx of qualified leads. Your ongoing nurturing of those leads most likely caused a rush of closed sales at the other end of the hose.

Where the water is in the hose needs to be taken into account when setting quotas for your sales staff. You want quotas that are challenging but realistic so that you are motivating rather than discouraging them as they work on filling that pipeline. Remember, your best sellers are goal-oriented, self-motivated types who like to get things done, so give them a task they can complete with satisfaction.

SHORTENING YOUR SALES CYCLE

Thankfully, there are additional steps you can take even with ideal clients to shorten your sales cycle without rushing or pressuring anyone.

1. Restructure the Offer

One of the best ways to shorten your sales cycle is to break your sale down into smaller pieces. This doesn't mean that you actually reduce the sale in the long run; you simply offer it in parts instead of as a whole. Breaking the sale into smaller pieces not only makes buyers less hesitant to sign on the dotted line, but it can also greatly simplify the approval process necessary to move forward.

Consider a situation where the approval process for a $300,000 sale requires a vice president-level approval and you're communicating with someone at the director level. Instead of relying on the director to get the sale approved by a vice president, you could break the sale into three $100,000 parcels. Assuming the director has the authority to approve a $100,000 decision, it enables you to close the sale much faster. You've removed an entire layer of the approval process.

2. Change Your Target

In the example above, you could shorten the sales cycle by opening communication initially with the vice president instead of the director. The VP may be able to approve the full $300K project.

3. Take the Path of Least Resistance

One of Carl's clients, "Dan," runs a franchise with a licensing fee attached. They were able to speed up their sales cycle by simply tweaking the procedure that prospective franchisees go through to become members. Dan used to ask prospects to attend an information seminar and then an orientation before they began the interview and approval process. During the approval process, he would have prospects speak to references (individuals who already owned franchises) about any questions they had regarding the business model.

After a while, Dan realized that the prospects got very excited when they talked to the franchise owners serving as references. He thought those interactions would actually have more value earlier in the process, so he started having the existing franchise owners come to the initial information meeting. He found that with this system, prospects were ready to make a decision much faster, greatly shortening the sales cycle. Sometimes a small tweak in the selling process can make a huge difference.

4. Circumvent the RFP

As we've already discussed, RFPs require a great deal more "paperwork" (and wait time) than other transactions. When you find yourself vying for an RFP, consider offering services or projects to the company that fall outside the RFP's scope. This is a way to get in the door faster, shorten your sales cycle, and put you in a stronger position to compete for the RFP.

For example, one of my clients in the promotional products industry targeted VPs and directors of marketing in liquor companies because they tend to buy such items in high volume. One liquor company VP said he had a contract in place with another vendor and the next review period was 6 months away. Many sellers would give up at this point. Big mistake. There is still opportunity here. We asked questions about any needs the company had that fell outside the RFP. The marketing department's hands were tied when it came to spending on promotional items due to the contract. But we uncovered that a number of other departments—communications, human resources, investor relations, meetings and events, and so on—were constantly buying promotional items, and their spending did not fall under the terms of the contract. They could buy from anyone. My client became a supplier to these departments, which was a shorter sales cycle (although in smaller volume than the marketing department). As we got closer to the review period for the marketing RFP, we made sure my client met individually with members of the decision-making team to start relationships and find out what was important to each one. That way, when they were ready to do the vendor review, my client was already a current vendor and was top of mind with the decision committee.

CARL'S COMMENTS:

One of my client companies sells medical devices and typically has a 12-month sales cycle. The devices are complicated and expensive, and the transactions often have to be approved by several layers of both health-care providers and administrators. One technique they were able to use to shorten their sales cycle was to talk through the contract with key decision makers and ask them, "If you were in front of the board right now, what would your recommendation be?" This enabled them to get a verbal agreement right away, rather than waiting months for the paperwork to make its way through the various departments.

As soon as they had the verbal agreement, they would email a basic contract to all concerned parties and ask for feedback. This way, by the time the buyers did all of their internal checks, the contract had already gone through its initial review. This strategy saved one to three months in the sales cycle, and it's a really good example of how understanding the buying process helps you adjust your selling process accordingly.

Carl's medical device client is a good example of how the approval process isn't completely linear: many steps are often happening all at once. For example, when writing this book, Carl and I didn't wait until we were finished writing chapter 12 to start thinking about cover art. We worked on both simultaneously. Always ask yourself if there is any way to take care of something earlier in the sales cycle and reduce the amount of time it takes you to close.

5. Sell Initial Consultations or Starter Kits

When the service you offer is very complicated and involves a large investment on the part of the client, you may want to offer an introductory package that allows the client to try out or sample your product or service. For example, one of my clients sells a big analytical service. For a long time they began the sales process with a discovery session where they used a large whiteboard to identify the issues their prospects were wrestling with.

This was a great selling strategy—it really gave prospects a feel for what they offered—but it also cost the company a lot of money. It involved preparation, travel, lodging, and meeting time. What's more, it would often result in a second whiteboard session to further refine the information so that it could be put into a proposal.

I helped the company repackage the whiteboard sessions into an initial consultation which they began to sell as a discovery product. This was a relatively low-cost, low-risk option that made clients eager to sign, and it ended up reducing their sales cycle by an average of two months. A very nice bonus was that the majority of discovery session clients signed up for the larger package because they were involved in identifying what they needed.

Of course, these strategies are mostly applicable to companies with relatively long sales cycles. Retail stores, restaurants, and other businesses with shorter sales cycles use different strategies, such as product positioning on shelves, to encourage customers to buy. The underlying principle at work is the same: examine closely how your customers buy and adjust your strategies accordingly.

DON'T ABANDON YOUR PIPELINE

As we've already stated, longer sales cycles can lead to fatigue with sellers, but abandoning good prospects often hands them directly to your competition. Staying conscious of your sales cycle helps you realize that the deal will eventually close, even if it's taking longer than you thought it would.

Efficiency is important, but it must be kept in perspective. Remember, even though you want to streamline your processes as much as possible, your buyer is a human being, not a robot. In fact, there are human beings at each stage of the buying process: reading your emails, listening to your phone messages, and signing off on the next stage of the RFP. And like all human beings, any of them may be unpredictable and subject to all kinds of changes of mood. Some are a little high maintenance and need lots of nurturing and reassurance. **But if that human being will make a good client one day, don't give up, because it's better to close a good deal slowly than to throw away a good deal quickly.** When it comes to keeping that pipeline full and flowing, "effective" trumps "efficient" every time.

THE FOUR BUYING STYLES

All those wonderful human beings you deal with during the selling process have unique personalities and preferences that affect the way they like to buy. This buying style determines how they are comfortable making a purchase, whether that means going into a wallet and shelling out personal money or signing a form that authorizes a sale to go to the next stage in their company.

There are four basic buying styles that govern how people like to purchase. While it's not uncommon to see a little bit of each style in yourself or your clients, everyone has a style that tends to dominate the others. Preparing for all four and tuning into your clients' dominant style will give you a decided advantage during the selling process.

Panthers Like to Pounce. Panthers are the decisive types who like to buy quickly. They tend to be demanding customers, but they don't want to drag the process out unnecessarily. They want to know the bottom line and move on. Carl likes to joke that panthers are often wrong but never in doubt.

Politicians Like Trends. You know those people who trade in their cars every six months and always have to have the newest cell phone? Those are politicians. They like to please people and promote themselves, so they need to be coaxed and even flattered a little. They want to know why buying from you is the best purchase possible. They want to feel like buying will make them look smart and that everyone in the company will think they're amazing for coming up with such a great resource. While panthers couldn't care less what others think, politicians need to know that other people are going to admire the purchase.

Protectors Like Tradition. Protectors like predictability and resist risk. They feel it is their job to protect the company, its vision, and by proxy all those who are committed to that vision. They need to see logical reasons why the purchase is in the best interests of the company, and they prefer products and services that are tried and true over those that are new and trendy. Protectors need a step-by-step sales process with a logical progression. When selling to protectors, keep things predictable or they will immediately pick up on the inconsistencies.

Professors Like to Analyze. Professors buy based on data. They take their time, and they don't have to like you personally to buy from you. They tend to resist actually making a decision so that they can do a little more research and look at a few more charts and graphs. They love hearing about your track record and the numbers that support it. They want to hear about how your other customers are doing and the ROI they are getting from you.

CARL'S COMMENTS:

One of my mentors is a typical "professor" type and often says, "Carl, I'd rather miss out on a good deal than get caught in a bad one." Personally, I'm a panther, so I'll buy on gut instinct and figure out the details later. I can fix anything!

Your prospects will leave you clues to their style in their interactions with you. The panthers are quick and results focused. The politicians want to make sure everyone is happy and that the purchase reinforces their elite status. The protector wants to know that the purchase is safe and sensible, and the professor wants to know that it's the highest quality with a proven track record. The better you prepare for and learn to recognize each type of buyer, the smoother your selling will go.

Understanding your sales cycle is not the most exciting part of business development, but it is absolutely essential to planning effectively. When you understand your sales cycle you will make the right decisions with regard to identifying your A-level clients, setting quotas for your salespeople, and selecting your business development initiatives. If you don't understand your true sales cycle, you will likely make the wrong decisions for each of these categories.

Remember, the ultimate goal is that when the prospect is ready to spend money, you are there to collect it. Understanding your sales cycle can give you the patience and perseverance you need to align your selling with your clients' buying. This is your path to the cash. Now that you know the direct route to selling more, the next chapter will help you figure out what to say to pique the interest of the right prospects.

CHAPTER 4

YOUR MESSAGE SUCKS

– Here's Why.

YOUR MESSAGE SUCKS
AND HERE'S WHY

An effective sales message captures the attention of prospects, makes them want to learn more about what you have to offer, and creates a sense of urgency. For example, what was your reaction to the title of this chapter? Did you notice it? Did it make you want to read further? Did you feel like you wanted to read it now? When you saw it in the table of contents, were you tempted to skip the other chapters and glance at this one?

If you answered yes to any of those questions, then the chapter title resonated with you, which is exactly what Carl and I designed it to do. We carefully considered several important qualities about our target readership, and we tested it with a sample of this population. We got some feedback, we tweaked it, and the fact that you just read it at the top of the page means we got it right.

Thus far, we've defined business development, learned how to plan it, and discovered how to incorporate a realistic sales cycle into that plan. In this chapter we will cover what you actually say to your prospects once you start implementing that plan. If your sales calls are not yielding the appointments and closings you desire, then your sales messaging probably sucks. But don't worry! This chapter will tell you why it sucks and how to fix it.

YOU GET ONE SHOT: NO PRESSURE!

While most of us need a second chance now and then in life, there are rarely second chances in business development. You can't call a busy vice president or CEO a second time and say, "Hey, our first conversation really didn't go the way that I wanted it to. Can we try that again?" The prospect has moved on, and you have no choice but to do the same.

While emails can only be judged by the responses they generate, it's not difficult to determine if your message is resonating when you're face to face with someone. Consider a networking event where you strike up a conversation with someone and share what you do. Does his face light up? Does he pull out his phone to put you in touch with someone who needs your product or service? Or does he smile politely with a glazed look in his eyes?

If the people you meet respond with attentiveness and referrals more often than not, then you are using the right message. If you're getting the glazed look or the polite dodge, you need to go back to the drawing board to discover the words and the phrases that will get you a better result.

There are a few common mistakes that can cause your messaging to suck. Sometimes a single word or phrase just needs to be tweaked slightly. Other times you may be making bigger, strategic messaging errors during the sales process.

Your Marketing Message Is NOT Your Sales Message

Many sales messages suck because they weren't developed for sales at all. A lot of organizations put a huge amount of time and resources into developing their marketing message and unique selling proposition (USP) and then assume that this can double as their sales message. But a marketing message is created to appeal to the masses, while a sales message must excite genuine interest during a one-on-one (or one-on-group) interaction. Too often companies don't have a sales message at all, so sellers create their own without guidance or oversight. This management blind spot leaves a vital component of the sales process completely to chance.

You get one shot with a prospect...

...so, no pressure!

When you're doing business development right, you have a carefully planned strategy to take your prospects through each step of the sales process. The goal in any given interaction is to move them from one step to the next. So it makes sense that the overarching marketing message for the entire company could not be same as the sales message that takes the prospect from one step in the relationship to the next. The most brilliant marketing message simply can't hit all the emotional and personal notes necessary to connect with individuals and help them move forward with you.

Right Message, Wrong Situation

A sales message designed for one situation will not necessarily work well in another. For example, you may have perfected your 30-second elevator speech (or "30-second commercial," as it's often called). This works great if you are actually in an elevator and have someone's complete attention. But it will get you those glazed looks if you try to work 30 seconds of monologue into a conversation in the buffet line at a networking event. Live, spur-of-the-moment dialogue requires a completely different approach (we call it "conversation ping-pong"), even if you include some of the same words and phrases. Sellers who have perfected their 30-second commercial often don't have dialogue prepared for the times they need it.

Identify the situational elements of your prospect interactions. Will it be in their offices? Will it be one-on-one or one-on-group? If it's likely to be a group setting, what are the roles of the people who will be there? Once you've answered these questions, you want to craft and prepare a message for each kind of interaction you expect to have. Some say they don't need to prepare a sales message because their prospects come to them by referral. If you think about it, those messages are twice as important to prepare, because someone has put his or her reputation on the line by recommending you. When contacting prospects by phone, you'll want to have an impactful voicemail message prepared. (Some people don't like to leave voicemails, but I see voicemails as an ideal opportunity to leave a one-on-one advertisement customized especially for your prospect. Not leaving a message is a missed opportunity.)

Regardless of the type of interaction, the wording is not something that should be left up to chance. You want to know exactly what you're going to say before you say it, so that the words you choose will be the right message for the right situation.

CARL'S COMMENTS:

Whenever someone is selling to me, I like to take the conversation a little deeper. If I'm buying clothes and the salesperson says, "Mr. Gould, that suit would look great on you," I'll often counter with, "Thank you! Why do you think so?" Unfortunately, salespeople are rarely prepared for these kinds of probing questions. Either they haven't thought their answers through, or they were told to push the brown suits and they're just following orders.

I find the same thing at restaurants. If I ask for a recommendation, the server will almost always tell me what he or she likes, rather than asking me about the kind of food I like. Whatever the sales situation, it doesn't take long for savvy customers to see that you are selling based on what works for you, not what works for them.

Leaving the Message to Chance

If you were throwing a dart and had one opportunity to hit the center of the target, would you want to throw it blindfolded? Of course you would rather have your eyes wide open and the lights on. Yet many salespeople approach their one opportunity with a prospect like a shot in the dark.

When a seller doesn't think through or plan the sales message in advance, there is a good chance that the message may not be strong enough to be impactful and take the prospect relationship to the next step.

Further, even if a seller prepares the message and practices ahead of time, that doesn't mean it should be delivered like a monologue. Asking prospects "high gain" questions during the interaction will help elicit information about their needs, wants, and priorities. You then pull from your prepared words and phrases to illustrate why what you're offering is of significantly more value (in a way that is meaningful to the decision maker) than what the competition is offering or than the prospect's current solution. When you're responding to what your prospect told you was important, you can present what you're selling as a perfect match. When you're reciting a monologue with no prior planning, it's a shot in the dark.

Many companies teach their sellers to use a targeted first sentence, but few ensure they are armed with the rest of the dialogue paths, including the exact questions that enable them to navigate to a desired outcome. Even fewer companies have their sellers demonstrate proficiency in using the right sales messaging and "high gain" questions for a particular situation. Those who do can be more confident that they are not taking a chance with their most important prospects.

MAKING THAT ONE SHOT COUNT

Now that we've covered the most common reasons why sales messaging sucks, let's talk about what we can do to make it effective.

Know the Lifetime Value of Your Prospect

The better you understand the potential benefit that an A-list client can offer your company, the more likely you are to take all the steps necessary to make that one shot count. As we've already emphasized, the right clients will buy from you over and over again, and they'll refer others. It's almost impossible to overstate their lifetime value.

Unfortunately, many sellers think only of the sale at hand, which can tempt them to take shortcuts or give up when things take an unexpected turn. Make sure your sales team is trained to think of the long-term benefits to both themselves and the company, so that they'll be willing to put in the extra work in the short term. And make sure the managers who support seller efforts are also thinking of the long term so that they are not tempted to encourage the wrong behavior.

Be Brilliant in Your Situational Messaging

Most of us are more comfortable in some settings than in others, but you want to invest the time and effort to become brilliant in each of your situational messages. You and your sales team can't be content to be great one-on-one but mediocre in front of a group or vice versa. Likewise, it doesn't make sense to be great in a meeting but not in the prospecting conversation that leads the decision maker to say yes to the meeting. You have to build on your strengths and strengthen your weaknesses, because you need to maximize every kind of opportunity to do business development right.

Understand the Emotional Side of Sales Messaging

Most of us tend to buy on emotion and rationalize the purchase afterward, so the emotional side of the sales message is one of its most critical components. The degree to which sales language takes this into account will separate those who do okay in closing sales from those who do exceptionally well.

I learned about the emotional side of sales messaging during my years on the decision-maker side of the desk, as a brand manager for a consumer packaged goods company. I was one of ten such managers, and my job was to do everything I could to increase market share, distribution, and sales. My future promotion depended on it. I frequently received calls from different kinds of sellers who wanted to provide me with various kinds of products and services.

Often I would get calls from two sellers working for competing companies. Each seller would have a different message, but the one with the better message got my attention. For example, Seller A's message might explain that he worked with a lot of companies like mine; maybe I'd keep his number, maybe I wouldn't. Seller B's message might say something like, "You know what? I've done some research and I have some insights for you that will help you increase market share, distribution, or sales in your category."

Now, what was important to me back then? I wanted to be promoted. To get promoted over my colleagues, I had to do something outstanding for my brand's market share, distribution, or sales, and Seller B was singing my song! Seller A explained what he did in general terms; Seller B basically told me he was the key to my promotion. Not only would Seller B get the meeting over Seller A, but I would also greet him with coffee and bagels!

Now the kicker here is that Company B might not even be as good as A. Company B got in because their seller said something that mattered to me. He hit the right emotional notes, and he couldn't have done it if he hadn't prepared strategically ahead of time. For an exercise on making your message more emotionally compelling go to www.BizDevDoneRightBook.com/whydoesitmatterexercise.com

CARL'S COMMENTS

Many successful salespeople aren't necessarily selling a groundbreaking or original product; they simply make the right emotional connection with the customer. In the 1983 comedy *National Lampoon's Vacation*, hapless husband and father Clark Griswold buys a hideous green station wagon with faux wooden side panels because the salesman keeps saying,

"Clark, this is your automobile, my friend. You deserve this. You've earned it!"

Of course, Clark's wife is horrified when he brings it home, and hilarity ensues, but the scene underscores the fact that hitting all the right emotional notes with a prospect is far more important than listing all the item's features and functions. The salesman got the sale not because of the car itself but because he connected with Clark and said what he needed to hear.

Make the Prospect a Rock Star

Effective marketing messages may focus on the features of your product or the advantages of your service, but effective sales messages make your prospect look and feel like a rock star. Even if you're a B2B seller and the buyers insist they are only concerned about the budget and the RFP, they will still have to answer for their purchase. They may get praised if the project goes well, but they will certainly get chewed out if something goes wrong.

In those situations, your goal is to take the risk off the table and help your prospects justify the purchase to their bosses. You are persuading them that buying from you will make them look like a rock star to the company. This means you'll need to know or make some assumptions about how they get reviewed. Your sales message will help them visualize explaining to their boss why you are exactly the right fit over any other potential solution while taking credit for how well the project has gone.

Avoid the Disconnect

One of the most important ways to make your sales messaging effective is to ensure that it communicates clearly. A disconnect is more damaging than a message that doesn't hit a home run emotionally, because there's nowhere to go from there. If your prospect doesn't understand beyond a shadow of a doubt what you do and why it's so important to take the next step with you—whether that's a meeting, reviewing a proposal, or closing the sale—your sales process is pretty much dead in the water.

There was a promotional products company (they imprinted logos on various products) I knew of that wanted to find language that would set them apart from all the other promotional products companies out there, so they decided to call themselves a "promotions company."

Unfortunately, this led to closed doors because, in the industry they were targeting, a "promotions company" was a company that put together promotional campaigns and events, not a company that put logos on products. To make matters worse, when they did get in the door, some prospects were confused (and sometimes angry) because what the company was offering was different from what they expected.

It is very important that you let your prospects know exactly what you do in language that is relevant and compelling to them and will bring them to that Moment of Yes®. We've all heard the saying that the "confused mind says no." If people aren't completely sure what you do or if you overwhelm them with information or language that isn't directly relevant to them, they immediately default to saying no. On the other hand, if you communicate in a clear and relevant way, you bring them closer and closer to saying yes.

Give a Clear Call to Action

Every interaction with your prospects is about guiding them to the next step of the sales process. This means you need them to be very clear about what they should do next to move forward with you.

For example, if you are working at a trade show, consider what action you want people to take when they walk by your booth. A catering company might want passersby to sample their food and beverage offerings. A consultant might want people to sign up for a follow-up appointment. Whatever the desired action is, the entire booth will be designed around that goal.

The same goes for any other interaction. If you're at a networking event and your goal is to secure a meeting with a prospect, don't confuse the interaction by trying to close a sale in that moment. Remember, your goal is just one step in the process. If you're on the phone, maybe you just want to find out the best address to send a prospect information. If you're in a group setting, maybe your goal is just to get everyone present to agree that a product or service like yours would be beneficial to them. Whatever the next step is for your sales process, make sure your communication builds up to and ends with a clear and singular call to action.

Email works the same way. In fact, when sellers aren't getting many responses to their emails, I often have them go back and reread them to see if they were clear about what they asked the prospect to do. Often they discover that they asked three different questions, asked no question at all, or gave five pieces of information, all of which most likely left the reader unsure of what to do next.

Suppose you have connected with a CEO's assistant who has offered to forward your information to his boss. Instead of sending a big wordy email, try starting with the sentence: "Thank you in advance for forwarding the information to [Name]" and then refrain from asking for anything else. From the very first sentence, the assistant knows exactly what to do with that email, and if you will need something else from him in the future, you can always send it in a separate email.

THE SLAM DUNK MESSAGE

The right message is all about the right words for the right target in the right situation. When crafting your sales message, you'll delve deeply into who your ideal clients are and what they need to hear. If you've got more than one target, you'll have more than one message.

The Right Message Repels the Wrong People

A prospect who ends up being a bad fit for your company can waste a lot of your resources and energy. But when you're doing business development right, you'll find that the right words for your ideal client will actually repel some of the wrong people. This saves you a great deal of time and effort.

Testing for Traction

A well-crafted sales message will bring a certain percentage of your prospects to the Moment of Yes®, but how do you determine what language will give you that kind of traction? My company does a great deal of research on the clients of our clients to determine just that. We study them to discover exactly what caused them to take the initial meeting or sign on the dotted line, whether they were changing vendors, choosing between competing bids, or deciding on a new solution.

Once we zero in on the words and phrases that bring prospects to that Moment of Yes®, we craft the sales language. (I prefer to call the message itself a springboard rather than a script, because life doesn't happen according to a script. The message needs to be a flexible tool that gets you to the next step.) Once we have the message, we test it in the market.

One of the worst business development mistakes you can make is to take a message live to high priority prospects without testing and tweaking to ensure you will get to that Moment of Yes® as often as you should. This costs time, money, and opportunities. During the testing process, we listen for that "aha!" moment during calls and watch for those eyes to light up in meetings, taking note of which words and phrases are helping us gain traction and which ones are falling flat.

Based on the testing results, we refine the message. Then (and only then!) we're ready to expand the business development effort. If we don't get the traction we expect, we go back and refine the message more until we are getting the right percentage of positive responses. This approach allows us to maximize the opportunities before us, instead of leaving too many on the table because we didn't take the extra time to get the wording just right.

It's very important that this data is gathered systematically from a wide sample of clients rather than from anecdotal evidence of individual sellers. Your sellers can and should give you feedback, but they may not fully understand why an interaction ended the way it did. As we've already noted, not every seller is a sales strategist, so you don't want to rely solely on their interpretation of events.

That means you'll need analysis from either an in-house sales strategist or a sales consultant known for crafting effective sales language to help you develop the precise messaging. When you do business development right, you perfect your message and roll it out strategically. This ensures that your sellers have a repeatable, predictable process for success.

Quality Control

Once you've crafted and perfected the right message, you will want to ensure that your sellers are using it effectively, not deviating to language that is off-strategy or defaulting to the language they used years ago. If they do, they could be wasting time and opportunities, so you will want to monitor your sales staff to be sure they are consistently using the language that you know will achieve results.

In addition to ensuring your sellers are utilizing the message to its fullest potential, certain industries will need quality control to ensure compliance with any industry regulations. Sellers who deviate may put the company at risk of legal action.

CARL'S COMMENTS:

A message that's a slam dunk in one market can be an air ball in another. Couple that with salespeople who don't buy into the message personally, and you've got a message that sucks.

Not long ago, I was working with a global company that was selling its product in 35 different countries, from the United States to Europe, and from South Africa to Australia. They would craft their sales messages from an aggregate of what was working all over the world. They had a few successful sellers in each market, so the executives would take whatever those high performers were saying and write it into the language for the global market.

When I started working with them, we began analyzing which messages resonated best in which market. We found that many sellers were emphasizing what was important to them personally but that those priorities weren't necessarily resonating in the market they were tasked to reach. Other sellers were being handed a script they didn't personally believe in, so the delivery was falling flat.

When I pointed this out to the company leadership, I was greeted with disbelief. So I conducted a body language test. When you believe in what you are saying, your voice is full and you tend to lean forward. We brought each team member to the front of the room and had them talk a little bit about the product, videotaping them for the CEO. Every single salesperson had their voices crack at some point and swayed side to side during their presentations—all indicators of conflicting feelings. Many even blushed.

The CEO was finally convinced of the problem. So we helped them recraft their sales messages to be market specific and trained their sales staff in each market to get them fully on board. These simple steps caused their closing ratios to double every year for the next four years!

The Power of the Slam Dunk Message

Sometimes the difference between almost the right language and exactly the right language is the difference between a shot that rims out and one that wins the game. When we start a Door Opener® program for any client, we begin with crafting their sales message. Before we met one of our clients, they used a sales message that conveyed that they saved their clients five dollars an hour on labor. These were a significant savings in their industry, and they were doing moderately well with this message.

Then we came in to analyze what language would "wow" their prospects and make them believe that a meeting with our client was essential, thus taking their message to the next level. Using the same math, we revised the message to convey that they saved one of their clients $15,000 per month with a strategic recommendation. Both statements were true, but the $15,000 message was a slam dunk while the $5 message wasn't. The company found that this more powerful message directly led to significantly more opened doors and more closed sales. Never underestimate the power of one small phrase change.

I've experienced the power of the slam dunk in my own business as well. One Friday afternoon after a particularly long week, I was sitting in my car outside Starbucks, looking forward to a much-needed latte. I had one more prospect to call: she had reviewed our proposal for the Door Opener® Service and loved what we had to offer, but she was struggling with the investment it would require.

When she answered my call, she explained, "Your service is everything I want and need, but I just can't bring myself to make the investment at this point in time. So I'm going to hold off. Let's revisit this again in a couple of months."

I was at that crossroads that every salesperson has experienced at one time or another: I could thank her and offer to check back in a couple of months, which would mean that I could go ahead and enjoy my latte. But I knew that the investment was still going to be a challenge for her in three months. Holding off until then would not do her or me any favors.

So I put off the latte. I reminded her of our original conversations and said, "You told me that sales growth is phenomenally important to you."

"That's right," she answered.

"You also told me that you have tried many other ways to open relationships with new decision makers and that you don't have the talent in-house to be able to get in the door with these prospects."

"Yes. That's right," she admitted.

"So if you need to have this growth, and you don't have anybody to help you to get it, how are you going to solve this problem?"

And then I shut up and let her think about what I had just said. And after a very pregnant pause, she said, "You're right. I have no way of doing this unless we move forward on this project together. Go ahead and send me that contract."

Just like we talked about in chapter 2, I didn't think of this answer to the objection on the spot. I had prepared for this phone call, and I knew that this objection was a possibility. After I asked the question that turned the situation from "not now" to "yes, let's get started"—a slam dunk—I had my latte.

Maintaining Control of the Conversation

The slam dunk message can get lost if the conversation takes a turn you're not prepared for. When sellers don't know what to expect in a given situation and are hit with something that they didn't anticipate, it can feel like a pop quiz in class. They may get nervous or even panic. Nothing good happens when sellers feel panic.

When you've gained experience in sales, you realize that there are only so many places the conversation can go. It's very rare that anyone will come up with anything outside a handful of objections, so there is really no need to get blindsided. When you're crafting your sales language, you'll consider each likely scenario and create a message that says what your prospect needs to hear. It is equally important to be prepared with the answers for the objections that will come your way.

This ensures your sellers will be very well prepared for the overwhelming majority of situations they encounter, enabling them to maintain control. Just going into an interaction with a good sense of what to expect and how to respond gives sellers greater confidence. And then they'll be better able to improvise for the tiny percentage of the situations that no one could possibly anticipate, because they're not improvising on everything else.

YOUR MESSAGE IS AWESOME

Once you understand clearly what your sales messaging is supposed to do, it's much easier to assess it accurately and determine what should be improved. Is your situational messaging brilliant, or is it just okay? Have you been using too much marketing language in sales situations? Are you creating a disconnect or cluttering your communication with too many calls to action?

If you're a new company and you're not sure where your messaging stands, then it's time to start testing it and see. You'll have a strategist—either in-house or from outside—weigh in and help you make an educated decision about what to keep and what to improve. Why spend so much time perfecting your marketing message yet spend no time at all on your sales message?

Sales messaging is never one size fits all. It has to be adaptable for the situation, for the audience, and for those little twists and turns the conversation can take. It needs to be loaded with emotional benefits that say what your prospect needs to hear. It needs to be tested and refined to bring prospects to the Moment of Yes®.

And once it is, you can stand back and say proudly, "My message is awesome."

CHAPTER 5

PROPER CARE

and

FEEDING

– of Your Pipeline.

THE PROPER CARE
AND FEEDING
OF YOUR PIPELINE

S o you've written your business development plan, you understand your sales cycle, and you're perfecting your messaging. How do you ensure it all translates into a steady pipeline of deals that close on a regular basis? This chapter will cover everything you need to know about feeding and caring for your pipeline in a way that ensures your prospects will move smoothly from initial contact to close.

We all know what a properly cared for child looks like: healthy, happy, and an endless source of joy (and exhaustion)! A sales pipeline is not too different. Take care of it, and it will bring you a steady stream of closed deals. Neglect it, and you'll find deals stalling and prospects losing touch. Some may even drop out of your pipeline altogether.

Just like parents are always thinking about dinner, driving someone to practice, or helping with homework, business development professionals are always calling, emailing, or networking with someone in their pipeline. When you're doing business development right, your schedule will be filled with prospects that you are steering through various stages of your sales process.

NURTURE YOUR LEADS

Caring for your pipeline means nurturing your leads so that they move from one step of your sales process to the next. As we discussed in the last chapter, this involves carefully planned messaging and relationship building. Suppose you've had a meeting with a prospect who doesn't need your services right away. What kinds of communication will deepen the relationship and move the prospect toward the close? Here are some examples of lead nurturing activities, ranked in order from shameful to most effective:

1. Bad: Not following up

The most basic crime of pipeline neglect is to not follow up at all. Throughout my career, I have been shocked at how many salespeople and business owners simply fail to follow up with someone when they don't close a sale in the time frame the seller wanted. As we've emphasized throughout the book, business development done right does not offer a lot of instant gratification. You may wish you got that check today, but you'll never get it if you don't follow up.

2. A little better: Leaving a check-in message or sending a quick email

Leaving a message for a prospect is better than not following up at all, but there's certainly room for improvement. A meaningful voicemail—as we discussed in the last chapter—can be a very useful tool. Unfortunately, too many salespeople suffer from the tick-mark syndrome we talked about in chapter 1: they leave a generic message that provides very little reason for prospects to move forward.

3. Even Better: Sending meaningful content

An even better example of lead nurturing would be to find an article that is relevant to your prospect and email it with a short cover note. The note would explain that you thought he or she might find the article interesting and express the desire to keep in touch. Although this won't necessarily move prospects forward in their thinking, it does give them something to think about.

4. Best: Deepening the relationship

An example of the best kind of follow-up would be sending the same article but including a different kind of note. This note would explain how the article applies to the issues that the prospect discussed with you during your meeting and how your company can help with that very challenge. The note would also offer a date and time to discuss how you can help the prospect in a specific way. Sending this kind of note means you've done some detailed thinking about your prospect and offered a communication that is content rich, deepens the relationship, and asks for a next step that offers benefit to the prospect.

Another example of taking the relationship forward is to invite your prospect to attend an important (important to your prospect, not necessarily to you), limited-access industry event with you. If some of your clients are present at the event, even better, as they will be able to spend time with your prospect singing your praises.

Recently I arranged for a client to address an industry association during a general session to make attendees aware of an exclusive member benefit: quarterly Sales Tele-Huddles (which I do for the association). This gave my client the ability to say a sentence or two about her company (about a quarter of people in the room are prospects of hers), help the association tout its member benefits to sponsors, members, and potential members, while at the same time providing exposure for me. A win-win-win. How did I dream this up? By thinking carefully about the people in my world (the person in the association who is looking for opportunities to increase membership and member satisfaction as well as my client who is looking for ways to open more prospect doors) and

The most basic crime of pipeline neglect...

...is to not follow up at all.

what would help them most. For a list of lead nurturing strategies, which actually nurture leads, go to www.BizDevDoneRightBook.com/leadnurturingstrategies.com

MONITOR YOUR PIPELINE

Part of caring for children is taking them to the doctor for regular checkups. The pediatrician measures their weight and height and checks other benchmarks to make sure they're growing as they should. If something is wrong—if they suddenly drop in the growth charts, for example—the doctor may order further tests to determine the reason.

Just like growth is natural for healthy children, movement is natural for a healthy pipeline. Your prospects should always be moving forward, not sitting still on your list. Once you know your sales cycle and the steps of your sales process, check your prospects regularly to see where they are in your pipeline. Anyone who stays in one spot for too long should raise a warning flag for you, just as it would if your child didn't gain any weight between checkups. Stagnation in your pipeline could signal that your messaging needs tweaking or that you need to offer content-rich ideas a little more often.

Movement in your pipeline is natural, because people like to buy, and they like to solve their problems. So while we do need to do certain activities consistently to keep our pipelines healthy, remember that the right prospects *want* to move through the pipeline. They're there for a reason: they need what you offer.

Don't Clog the Pipeline!

People will be ready to buy at all different times, and sometimes a business development professional that isn't paying enough attention can unintentionally get in the way of the purchase. Not long ago, my company decided to switch email providers, and we had some technical issues that needed to be solved before we could move forward. I'm not a technology expert, so I called the company we wanted to switch to for help. I got on the phone with someone who was very knowledgeable. But while he was able to answer some of my questions, he didn't give me all the information I needed. Instead he offered to send me some links to further educate me on the technology. I told him I was not a technology person, but he was eager to get me off the phone and onto the email list.

After the call, I received a steady stream of emails—twice a week like clockwork—to educate me on the service they offered. I was ready to buy, but the company was still trying to educate me. My company remained stymied for months, because I was busy and didn't have time to click on links and figure everything out on my own. What this seller's manager didn't know was that a good prospect got very frustrated, and they lost a sale that could have easily closed.

What could the salesman have done to avoid this? He could have simply asked me, "Caryn, what do you need in order to make a decision to move forward today?" I would have then been able to tell him exactly what I needed, and I would have happily written him a check right there. He would have gotten a sale, and I would have been able to check an important task off my list. But instead, I was stuck with a deluge of generic emails that were supposed to nurture me as a lead. Not only did they not nurture me, in the end they sent me to the competition, who was willing to answer my questions and sell to me the way I wanted to buy.

This experience also highlights a newer reality about selling: most of the time when prospects initiate contact with you, they've already checked out your website and researched your competitors. It's important to note that the right sales process for inbound leads will be a little different than the right process for outbound. Qualified prospects who put themselves into your pipeline deserve special attention; they may be ready to close faster than you think.

A Client Now or a Client Later

Years ago I knew a salesperson, "Kevin," who had a nice conversation with a decision maker who was buying from one of Kevin's competitors at the time. At the end of the conversation, the decision maker said, "I really appreciate you coming in. I'm glad I learned about your company. But to be quite honest, I'm going to stay with my current solution right now. But thanks again."

Kevin was so annoyed that the conversation didn't turn into a sale that he never called the prospect back again. This was a tremendous opportunity missed. The decision maker was not rejecting Kevin personally, and in fact she had indicated that she wanted to stay in touch. Something could have been going on with the current vendor that wasn't enough to make the decision maker change her mind that day, but who knows what might happen in a couple of months? Since Kevin never called, he'll never know.

Kevin could (and should) have called her back just to see how things were going. Instead he just let the relationship go, wasting all the time and effort he put into getting in the door and having the meeting. She was a qualified prospect who needed what he had to offer and was interested in learning more. He was irritated that she wasn't ready to buy when he was ready to sell, and he let his emotions ruin a potential relationship.

When you're properly caring for your pipeline, you view all qualified prospects as clients: the only question is whether they'll be your clients now or your clients later. This idea has profound implications for how you treat each prospect. Most of us have heard of psychologist Robert Rosenthal's famous 1964 experiment where he told elementary school teachers that their classes were comprised of extremely gifted students, when in fact the students in the classes had been selected at random. The teachers taught all the children as if they were gifted, and therefore the students learned more. The point is that the mind-set of the practitioner (in one case the seller and the other case the teacher) can change the outcome of the process.

In the same way, if you treat prospects with the care and attention that you would treat someone who was already your client, in the long run you'll see very different results than Kevin did. It might take several months or even a year for them to be ready to make a decision or a change. But when they're ready to move forward, you'll have built up enough trust and rapport to be in their decision set.

The Paradox of the Properly Cared for Pipeline

To do business development right, you need to be prepared for two extremes: the prospect that takes forever and the prospect that is ready to close this minute. The good news is that if you're ready for these two scenarios, you'll be ready for everything in between. Paradoxically, the better you're prepared for the extremes, the more you'll find that your pipeline as a whole will settle down and you'll be able to plan according to your normal sales cycle.

Preparing for extremes stabilizes your pipeline because you don't push the reluctant prospect and you don't slow down the eager prospect. You align the way you sell with the timeline that makes your prospects most comfortable, which cuts down on all the friction in the sales cycle that we discussed in chapter 3. If you're just as happy to nurture people along for a few more months as you are to sign them today, you'll meet far less resistance from everyone.

Avoid Ultimatums

When you're properly caring for your pipeline, you look at the sales process from your prospects' perspective, not just your own. One of my clients wanted to sell to the corporate office of a large hotel chain, because her office was right next to theirs. Unfortunately, my client's outreach wasn't greeted with the response she'd hoped for. She left a couple of messages, and they didn't get back to her right away. Although I mentioned the possibility that the prospect might not feel as strongly about being her client as she felt about signing them, she repeated her conviction that they should do business with her because of their location.

After not hearing back for a few more weeks, she told me she planned to leave one last message that would say, "Look, I've left a couple messages. We're clearly a good choice because we're right down the street. But if I don't hear back from you, I'm just going to assume that you're not interested." This was a classic example of a salesperson seeing the sales process solely from her perspective. She was ready to sell to them now, but they were not remotely close to being ready to buy. I explained that she was creating completely unnecessary friction with the prospect. What if they had simply been busy and unable to return her call? They may have been moving through her pipeline slowly, but after a message like the one she was about to leave, they wouldn't be in her pipeline at all.

DEEPEN THE RELATIONSHIP

All the activities that move people from point A to point B in your pipeline are those that deepen your relationships with them. So when you're thinking about the emails, voicemails, and other interactions, remember that your prospects are people. They go to work for a reason, and they have goals and struggles just like everyone else. Think about how they will perceive what you say and write. Will it push them away like my client's ultimatum, or will it deepen the relationship? The stronger your connection with prospects, the more smoothly they'll move through your pipeline. Take a few extra minutes to make the communication meaningful. You'll never be sorry you took the extra time, but you'll often be sorry if you don't.

CARL'S COMMENTS:

It's a small world, and it's getting smaller. Not too long ago, I was having dinner with the former CEO of a well-known recreational vehicle company. We were talking about competitive advantage, and he mentioned a software package the company had purchased over 40 years ago that had given them a huge edge at the time. About a week later, I recounted the story to my dad, a semi-retired computer networking professional. It turned out my dad had been the one who worked with the CEO on that very software project. He never would have imagined that the CEO would be having dinner with his son four decades later. You never know how or when a connection could come back around in your life.

When you take the time to nurture your pipeline, you're also building brand equity in the best possible way. My husband is in business development as well, and he has a lot of very strong relationships with both the people who have bought from him over the years and those who haven't. Recently, a man, "Tim"—who had never bought from him— was laid off and was looking for a job. When my husband found out, he got Tim an interview with one of his clients. My husband did this out of the goodness of his heart and because he genuinely cares about Tim. But think about what happens when you take care of people that way over the years. Most will be looking for a way to help you out in the future.

In the grand scheme of things, if you genuinely care about the people in your pipeline, they'll have plenty of good reasons to keep moving forward. You'll give them reasons to buy from you, to give you 100 percent share of sale, and to refer you often. This starts with simply being kind and considerate and continues with providing value and even going the extra mile, like my husband did with Tim. I believe that if you focus on the health and depth of your relationships, the money follows.

Hang In There

As we said way back in chapter 1, business development is purposeful and deliberate. Dollars will be awarded to the business development professionals who are patient and willing to hang in there until the prospect is ready to buy. I meet a lot of business owners with a stack of what I call "no-go" proposals: proposals they submitted to prospects who didn't end up selecting them. Yet they have never called those prospects back to see how things are going, which is a big missed opportunity. Vendor relationships don't always work out, so stay in touch.

As we discussed in chapter 3, sometimes you connect too late in a prospect's buying cycle, so you don't have enough time to establish trust before the decision has to be made. Following up, even when you weren't selected, allows you to build trust and nurture the relationship so that the next time they are ready to buy, you will be there to collect. That's also why it can be better to introduce yourself before a need arises. This takes the pressure off. They get to know you, you get to know them, and you establish trust, so when the opportunity is on the table you're the first one they call.

Leverage Your CRM

Various technological solutions exist to help you deepen your business development relationships. Numerous customer relationship management (CRM) programs and applications, many of which can be run from your phone, can play an invaluable role in nurturing your leads and keeping them moving through your pipeline. They can help you keep track of prospects' birthdays and anniversaries, as well as remind you to follow up with people in the time frame they requested and you promised. Of course, the software won't create the winning message for you, but it can help you stay on track with ongoing, productive communication.

I'm often asked to recommend a particular CRM, but I believe the best system for you is the one you'll use consistently. It's like the old debate about the treadmill, exercise bike, or elliptical machine. You can debate their merits for hours, but at the end of the day, the one that works best is the one you use consistently.

Several years ago, I was reaching out to a decision maker in a pharmaceutical company who was in the middle of a corporate reorganization. We talked about all sorts of things, including the abused dog she had just adopted who was afraid of his water bowl. At the end of the conversation she asked me to follow up with her in six months.

I took very careful notes on everything and set a date for the follow-up in my CRM. Six months later, I called her back. We started chatting again, and I asked how her dog was doing. "I can't believe you remember that!" she exclaimed. The dog was doing much better, and we moved on to talk about the reorganization and set a date and time for a meeting. Had I not taken those detailed notes, set the reminder for the follow-up call, and been able to pull up the information I needed, I might not have remembered the right time to call, let alone to ask about her dog and the water bowl. She was so touched that I cared enough to remember what we'd talked about. The conversation built trust between us and paved the way for a long-term relationship.

Honey, Tea, and Potato Chips

Sometimes you can deepen a relationship with simple caring advice. I once got to know the assistant to an executive, because I was working to get a client in the door with the assistant's very busy boss. She and I ended up having many conversations, and one day when she answered the phone, I noticed she had a scratchy voice. Of course that would be an inconvenience for anyone, but I knew firsthand that when you spend all day on the phone, a scratchy voice can make 8 hours of work feel like 50.

So when I heard her struggling to clear her throat, I told her about one of my personal remedies. "Try tea with honey and potato chips," I suggested.

"Wow," she said. "I've never heard that one before." I explained that the honey in the tea and the grease from the potato chips really help coat the throat and can buy you a few more hours on the phone. Of course, I kept good notes about our conversation in my CRM, and a couple of weeks later when it was time to call back, I asked her if it worked. She said it did, but more than that she was just touched that I cared about her enough to offer the advice and remember to ask how she was doing. She also ended up being very instrumental in getting the meeting for my client.

In the dynamic and often hectic world of business development, caring for your pipeline often comes down to these little moments when you can connect meaningfully with another person. It's about focusing on those people—their needs, their situations, their challenges—and offering thoughtful solutions that help them.

Caring for your pipeline involves making enough of these deposits into a prospect's emotional bank account (as Stephen Covey would say) so that when they are ready and able to buy, they choose you. You want to nurture them through with productive and purposeful communication that brings value. And if you do this, you will avoid the feast/famine syndrome that many sellers face.

CHAPTER 6

THE
NO
B.S.
SALES
HIRE

– Not All Salespeople Are Created Equally.

THE NO BS SALES HIRE

You can write an extremely detailed business development plan, understand your sales cycle thoroughly, and have perfect messaging. However, if you don't find the right people to execute that plan, navigate the sales cycle, and deliver the message, you still won't get the results you're looking for. Many business owners hire sales staff and then fire them after things don't work out as they had hoped. Were these bad sellers who gave "BS" answers in their interviews, or were the hiring managers not quite sure what to look for?

In fact, every company is different, and a salesperson that's a perfect fit at one company may be a bad hire at another. This chapter will teach you how to assess what kind of sellers you need, how to ask the right questions to find them, and how to persuade them to come work for you.

KNOW YOUR NEEDS

There are many people selling successfully for other companies who will not necessarily sell well for you. I worked with a newer company in the meeting planning industry once, and they spent well into six figures to hire a top-performing salesperson away from the market leader. They were very excited for him to use his existing relationships to get them lots of large accounts. The salesperson came in expecting to settle into the same routine he'd had with his previous employer. Both the company and the salesperson had a rude awakening.

The company soon learned that the high-level relationships the salesperson spoke about during his interview belonged to upper-level executives in his previous company, not to him. The salesperson discovered that there was a big difference between selling for the market leader versus the underdog. Without the name recognition of the industry heavyweight, the seller had to approach prospects in a completely different way. He had no experience with this and was like a newbie, trying to figure it out as he went and often getting it wrong. It was an expensive learning experience for both the company and the seller. There's an old adage that states, "The stronger the brand, the weaker the sales team; the weaker the brand, the stronger the sales team."

Unfortunately, it took this company nearly a year and a half to face the reality that this salesperson was not a good fit. Eighteen months of lost sales, missed opportunities, and over a hundred thousand dollars invested into a hire that wasn't the right fit from the start. Worse, the connections he did make weren't the right connections for them. And when the company finally let him go, they had to hire a new person and start all over again. It was a painful lesson for everyone concerned.

This situation didn't happen because the salesperson was a bad seller. On the contrary, he was incredibly effective when working for an industry leader. But the skill set and experience that made him so successful there did not translate well into working for an underdog company. Similar problems can surface with successful sellers who move from a company where the sales process is meticulously documented, with training provided, to a company where sellers are expected to figure things out for themselves. A seller who has thrived in a highly structured system with precise tools (such as significant managerial oversight, support people in place to relieve sellers of administrative responsibilities, and documented sales messaging) may not be able to be successful in an environment without those things in place.

To hire the right salesperson the first time—without wasting valuable months and dollars figuring out that you have to start over again—you need to hire a seller who fits where your company is right now. This is different from hiring support staff. If you're preparing for growth, it's a good idea to hire an office manager, a director of operations, or a health and safety officer with experience at larger companies, because they can help you navigate expansion. But you need sellers who can increase your sales now and operate successfully in your current environment, not sellers who will be a good fit in a couple years when you've drastically increased your market share.

CARL'S COMMENTS

Several years ago, I went for a golf lesson with a pro. "Carl, today I'm going to teach you two things," he explained. "I'm going to teach you the swing of the best player in the world, and then I'm going to teach you your swing." I wasn't sure if this was a compliment or not.

He videotaped me swinging a number of times, and then we sat down at his computer. He showed me Tiger Woods (then in his prime) swinging, and then he explained that I had a different physique, which caused my body to move differently. He explained how my swing would look with ideal execution:

different from the greatest player in the game but still very effective. We can approach a sales hire the same way. You may not be able to hire the best salesperson on the planet, but if you accurately assess your resources, your stage of development, and your growth trajectory, you can find the ideal seller for where your company is right now.

HIRE WELL THE FIRST TIME

Most of us who've been in business for a while have made a bad hire. If it's an accountant or a receptionist, you can usually recover pretty quickly. Larger companies can also absorb the costs of a bad hire without too much trouble. But a bad sales hire at a small- to midsized company can be a disaster. Your sellers are your ambassadors, and they generate your revenue. Here are some steps and strategies to help you get it right the first time:

Define the Perfect Hire Based on Your Needs

As we've already mentioned, the qualities and skills of the perfect sales hire will differ from company to company, even within the same industry. In addition to your market share and how structured your sales process is, you'll need to consider what you already have. For example, there are some companies that get a lot of qualified leads from SEO, so they just need a person who can turn those leads into closed sales. As we've discussed in earlier chapters, the skills needed to develop that initial relationship and close the deal are different from those needed to open the door in the first place.

You also want to consider what you already have in your personnel. I met a business owner, "Janice," who was in the audience at one of my presentations on how to get in the door with prospects. She told me how she had just fired a salesperson because he wasn't good at closing, although he was great at getting them in the door. I asked her if she had anyone in her company who *was* good at closing, and she explained that in fact she and her partner were great closers. Then I asked her what her company needed to be successful. She answered, "We need to break into new markets and create new relationships." Unfortunately, she had just fired the very person who held the key to their success. He wasn't the "perfect" salesperson, but he was a perfect fit for what they needed right then. What a waste.

Write a Slam Dunk Job Description

How will potential candidates know what you're looking for if you don't tell them directly? The best job descriptions are clear and specific. For example, if you're looking for someone who can establish a territory from scratch, don't just ask for an experienced salesperson. Explain that candidates will have to demonstrate that that they have developed a multimillion-dollar sales territory from nothing. If you are targeting particular kinds of accounts, specify that you are looking for a salesperson with a track record of developing them.

General requirements like "ten years of experience" can mean very different things. Does the candidate have ten years of experience taking over somebody else's accounts or ten years of experience initiating relationships where none existed before? Those two candidates will bring very different skill sets to the table. The more detailed your job description, the more qualified the pool of candidates you'll attract. Further, the better job description will repel candidates who are not a good fit.

Use Slam Dunk Interview Questions

Once you have your description written, you'll want to distribute it not just with an ad in the paper but through LinkedIn, to colleagues in your network, and even to your customers. Then it's time to develop the questions that you will ask each candidate to determine if they are a good match. There is a big difference between generic interview prompts ("Describe your strengths") and the types of questions that will actually tell you what you need to know.

For example, if you're looking for someone who can initiate relationships with no previous connections, you might ask: "Describe a situation where you've gotten a meeting with a prospect when neither you nor your employer had a previous relationship with that prospect. What did you do to get started?" As they answer, you'll be listening for someone who can describe a methodical process in great detail. The right seller will be able to tell you specifics about challenges he faced and how he overcame them to achieve success. For a list of interview questions for hunters who are door openers, go to www.Biz-DevDoneRightBook.com/hiretherighthunter.com

Although the right questions go a long way

A better job description will repel candidates...

...who are not a good fit.

toward cutting out the BS responses from unqualified candidates, some salespeople will still be able to offer plausible sounding answers that can lead you to think they are the right fit when they are not. Unless you have personal experience with the process you are asking the candidate to describe, it can be challenging to separate the authentic experiences from the BS answers.

In these cases, some companies find it useful to bring in outside help. My company has worked with many business owners to create accurate and specific job descriptions, develop the right interview questions, and assist with the final interviews. Our knowledge of the sales process helped our clients distinguish genuine answers from the BS to determine who was the best fit.

Pay Attention to the Minutia

Recently, we were interviewing for a Door Opener® position. There were two excellent candidates we were considering for an assignment. They both had similar skill sets and the same amount of experience, and both interviewed well. How did we choose? We asked for samples of emails they had sent prospects from previous sales positions. One had clearly taken the time to research her prospect's situation and wove what she learned into a short, concise email. It used compelling language, specifying why a meeting would benefit the prospect and offering dates and times—a clear call to action. The other candidate's email was very long, was not customized for the prospect in any way, and didn't include an "ask." Even worse, it used the phrase "squarely focused" (referring to her company's area of concentration) twice. Can you guess who got the job?

It's important to note that the person who wrote the poor email can be trained to write a better email. Certain deficiencies are fixable.

You just need to know where the land mines are and be honest with yourself about whether they may impede your sales success.

Benchmark the Position, Not the Personality

You always want to benchmark the sales position—the skills and experience you're looking for—and not someone's personality or style. When hiring, it can be very tempting to look for carbon copies of your highest-performing salesperson instead of looking for specific technical and interpersonal skills. But this often has unintended consequences.

CARL'S COMMENTS:

Not long ago I worked with a company that had built its entire sales team around their top performer. She was the first salesperson they hired, and they included her in their hiring, training, and recruiting processes for the rest of the sales staff. When my company was brought in to consult, we administered to the entire team a situational sales assessment that measures six areas of sales excellence. The top performer scored very well in four areas and very poorly in two. Interestingly, the other 16 people scored very poorly in those same two areas. This meant that the team as a whole had some glaring weaknesses.

This is exactly the risk you run when you use a person as your benchmark instead of the requirements of the position itself. This particular salesperson was the top performer because she had a specific set of skills, and she was able to use her unique personality to compensate for her weaknesses. Other people she helped to hire didn't necessarily share her ability to do that.

As Carl's story illustrates, top performers become top performers by utilizing their unique combination of skills and personality traits. Some perform well because they've been with the same company a long time, which has allowed them to develop strong relationships with a particular group of clients. Benchmarking the position instead of the person helps you hire team members whose strengths and weaknesses balance one another.

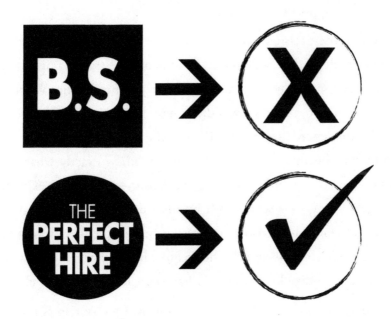

Survey the Stakeholders

Just as we study our clients' customers when we're crafting and perfecting their messaging, it can also be useful to get customer input on the sellers themselves. Why not ask your best customers why they said yes to the particular seller they were working with? Getting some feedback about what made the relationship work in the first place can provide vital insight into what to look for in new hires.

Assess Your Management Structure

As we've already said, if your sales process—from door opening to closed deal—is not carefully spelled out for the sales team, you will need to hire people who can be successful without that kind of supervision and support. On the other hand, if you have your process and messaging clearly documented, along with a manager who has time to supervise, you may be able to hire junior-level salespeople and give them the support they need.

Often the decision will come down to whether you want to hire an inexperienced person and invest a lot of time training or an experienced person who can already do what you need done. When my own business began to grow, I didn't have time to train and supervise an inexperienced person. So I hired the person who replaced me in my last business development job. She knew exactly what to do and required very little management. As our company has expanded further, hiring very senior-level business development professionals (most of whom have also held decision-maker roles in corporations) became our business model. They require little management supervision, because they know exactly what to do and they do it well.

This system has worked very well for us. One system is not necessarily better than the other, but you need to accurately assess the strength of your company's management structure and its implications for hiring.

ENTICE THE SALES TEAM YOU WANT AT AN AFFORDABLE PRICE

Once you've found the right candidates, how do you get them to work for you without breaking the bank? We could write an entire book on compensation plans, but for now we'll just look at the basics:

Find Out What They Want

It's very important to learn (ideally during the interview process) what kind of compensation package candidates are currently receiving and what they are looking for. You will need to get a feel for their expectations regarding the ratio of base salary to commission and bonuses. Some salespeople are used to working on 100 percent commission, while others would never consider it. Both types could be good at their jobs, but one will require a higher up-front investment from you.

Do the Math for Them and Show Them the Money!

It is possible that you will not be comfortable offering the base salary that desirable candidates require. How do you get them to consider working for you anyway? Show them the money! Do the math for them and show them how easy it will be for them to earn the income they are looking for. If possible, show them other examples of sellers from your company who have been able to get to that number (or more) and how they did it. Understand that some sellers may have been burned by previous employers who overpromised and underdelivered. This may have significantly reduced the amount of money the seller could earn and was completely outside his control.

Don't assume that just because the candidates are very high performing that they understand exactly how the compensation package works. Even if you think you've laid it out in a very straightforward way, take the time to run the numbers for them to be sure they understand what it would look like in real scenarios. I've been surprised to see how many high-level salespeople just do the best job they can without fully understanding how they're compensated. This often prevents them from maximizing their money and money for the company.

A salesperson switching industries or localities may not know how easy or difficult it will be to reach certain benchmarks in their new market. If you can show them on paper and with real-life examples how easy it will be for them to reach their goals, they are more likely to accept a lower base pay.

Mind the Incentives

Sellers behave the way they get paid. You want to make sure your compensation plan is incentivizing the activities you want and attracting the right kind of seller. For example, one company I knew of gave their sellers rewards for booking meetings. After they'd booked a certain number of meetings, they got rewards for every meeting thereafter. However, the company never bothered to define clearly what a "meeting" was.

I knew plenty of sellers at that company who would drop off a gift certificate for a manicure/pedicure for a prospect and record that as a meeting. They would do the same when they took somebody out for a quick cup of coffee that didn't produce a result. They were doing what they needed to do to get the incentive, but the incentive wasn't structured properly by management. It didn't encourage the behavior the company really wanted.

Creative Solutions

You want to hire the best people, but your sales costs cannot be so high that they prevent you from making a profit. The candidate with the perfect skill set who will make you unprofitable is still not the right fit.

One of my client companies wanted to hire a particular level of seller and thought they'd found the perfect candidate. She had ten years of business development experience in their category, she had held decision-maker positions, and she interviewed very well. A perfect fit, they thought. The only problem was the salary she required was far beyond what would produce an ROI for them.

We suggested that they seek out someone with a similar skill level—maybe not quite as high as their ideal candidate—who was willing to work part time. This strategy allowed the company to hire someone with the skills they needed to achieve success but at an investment level that made financial sense. With the right candidate, a part-time or work-at-home solution can be a win for the employee and a win for the company. This is just one example of a creative solution.

You may also be able to entice highly qualified candidates (who are asking for more than you can offer) by making it clear that you will not weigh them down with non-sales-related responsibilities. Many candidates can be persuaded to accept lower base pay if they are confident you will actually allow them to focus on selling rather than filling out spreadsheets and reports or training other sellers to be better. The most effective sellers prefer to work in the most streamlined way possible, so that they can make the most money for themselves and for you.

Counting the Cost

Every hiring decision has a cost, including the decision not to hire at all. You can hire a lower-level person to save some money in salary. But if you don't have the structure in place to support him or her, the hire ends up costing you a lot more than the money you've saved. A bad hire will cost money in lost sales, wasted opportunities, training time, and worst of all, damaged reputation. As we've said, your sellers are the ambassadors for your company, and if they're not doing their job well they can really hurt your brand.

The cost-to-benefit ratio for a particular hire will be different for every company and will depend on many factors, including your industry, market share, and management structure. Not hiring at all is often a big mistake, too: you miss out on opportunities and limit your growth. If you're not selling to your prospects, someone else will.

You're not looking for the perfect person; you're looking for the right person *for you*. Hire the best person you can the first time around so that you can maximize your opportunities and minimize the BS in your life.

CHAPTER 7

CHECKLIST for SELLERS

– You Know Your Seller is a Rockstar When…

YOU KNOW YOUR SELLER IS A ROCK STAR IF...

Even after the no BS hire, some salespeople don't work out the way they're supposed to. As we discovered in the last chapter, a bad hire can cost you time, money, and relationships, especially if it takes a while to figure out you made a mistake. Sellers with magnetic personalities, a rolodex full of names, and an enviable LinkedIn profile can be very charming, but they are not necessarily the rock stars you need. How can you assess your sales staff accurately and promptly, so that you don't have to wait a year to make necessary adjustments?

In this chapter, you'll learn how to recognize rock star seller attributes and behaviors. You'll also learn how to support them so that they feel encouraged and appreciated. You'll be able to incentivize the behaviors you want and discourage what you don't want, so that your sellers stay focused on bringing the maximum number of new dollars to the company.

THE ROCK STAR SELLER CHECKLIST

They do the right behaviors that move the sale forward.

Rock star sellers engage in productive behaviors that keep sales moving forward. Here are just a few examples of those "right behaviors".

They develop a target group of prospects based on company priorities. Their target takes into account the size of the initial sale but also the margin level and referral potential down the road.

They pursue the right prospects in the right places. These places could include networking events, trade shows, leveraging relationships, even outbound prospect calling. Pursuing the right prospect in the wrong place wastes valuable time, but rock star sellers know where to look.

They keep track of their leads effectively, whether with a CRM or a spreadsheet. They keep careful notes and refer back to them before each new communication with the prospect.

They contact their prospects at the right frequency. The seller who waits four months to follow up with a prospect has to start the relationship over each time. Rock star sellers effectively use voicemail, email, regular mail, and face-to-face meetings to follow up at the appropriate intervals. Rock star sellers also develop relationships with those who surround their prospects, including assistants, direct reports, and superiors. That way when they can't reach their prospects directly, they are still able to work the open lines of communication. And, when their prospects leave for different jobs, their relationships with prospect companies continue.

They demonstrate proficiency in the company's sales messaging and answers for objections at each phase of the sale. Rock star sellers assume that the prospect will have questions throughout the process, and they're well versed in what those questions might be and how to respond. On the rare occasions when they are confronted with an objection they didn't anticipate, they are not only skilled but also intuitive when thinking on their feet.

Most sales managers and the business owners keep a watchful eye on the end of the sales process, because that's where the money shows up. They may forget that all those closed sales (or lack thereof) are the result of the beginning and the middle of the sales process, not just the end. Lower sales don't necessarily indicate a problem with the closing procedure or its execution. The issue is often elsewhere in the pipeline, with identifying the right decision makers, delivering the message, or answering an objection effectively. To enable your sellers to reach rock star status, I always recommend companies put together a messaging and objections manual and provide it to sellers as part of their onboarding package. You can save a lot of time and make the most of each opportunity by documenting your sales messaging, live dialogue, and answers for objections. You can offer ideal wording for voicemails to leave during cold calls, warm calls, and referral calls, as well as what to say in networking situations: both live dialogue and the 30-second "elevator pitch." This is not to be thought of as a script but rather a springboard for conversation. Sellers need to know the words and phrases that are most compelling to the right decision makers. Any new objections your sellers encounter then get recorded and added to the manual so that each new salesperson gets the benefit of everyone else's experiences.

Then, instead of having sellers just read the manual, use role play to have them demonstrate proficiency. Once they've done this, you can send them out on your behalf with the confidence that they are maximizing the potential with their leads. Rock stars don't practice on the company's most important prospects; they master the messaging ahead of time.

They smoothly bring the sale to a close. Depending on the kind of sale, there could be a hundred different ways to close it. Rock star sellers use their own unique personalities and styles to take the straightest possible path from initial contact to close. Less effective sellers may wander off the direct path, lengthening the sales cycle unnecessarily. Once you have documented the messaging and understand your realistic sales cycle, look for rock star sellers to hit the benchmarks you expect. Don't worry if they don't all reach them by the same methods.

If salespeople aren't hitting the benchmarks you expect, start looking at the details that led up to the benchmark.

They ask for and get next steps at every phase of the sales process. Not long ago, one of my company's Door Openers® encountered an objection from a prospect that we hadn't specifically prepared her for. Instead of panicking, she responded confidently, "That's exactly why we should be speaking." Then she offered two sentences about why the prospect should take the next step with her. These sentences were so compelling and she was so proficient in delivering them that the prospect wanted to take the meeting with her, despite his objection.

Even good sellers can get distracted or bogged down, but rock star sellers ask for and get the next step at every stage of the sale. They don't get rattled when the conversation takes an unexpected turn, and they don't confuse the prospect with too many calls to action. They patiently and persistently bring the prospect to that Moment of Yes®.

They follow up methodically and immediately no matter what: no dropped balls. Each deal moves forward at its own pace, which means that you will sometimes have a large number of prospects requesting proposals or meetings at the same time. For example, if you have a great door-opening program, you'll soon have a swarm of prospects requiring follow-up. Under these circumstances, it's easy for one or two to get lost in the shuffle. Rock star sellers respond to situations like this by following up methodically and immediately, minimizing bulges in the pipeline. They fulfill their follow-up promises on time. If they can't get a proposal to the prospect by the promised date, they will contact the prospect and let him know when to expect it. They know that details in the business development process matter. Every fulfilled promise builds trust. Every missed promise destroys trust.

Sellers need to know the words and phrases that are most compelling...

...to the right decision makers.

Rock stars know how to work through the occasional dry spell. They stick to the process and message. Poor sellers may deviate from the process or messaging manual when they have a few disappointments. But rock star sellers will respond to these kinds of challenges by continuing to work methodically through their list of prospects. They understand that a few setbacks don't mean you should change the entire game plan or give up.

They customize their approach to the decision maker and the situation. Rock star sellers make the company message their own and are able to customize their approach to the buyer and the situation. When I was 23, I went to look for a car. I was living away from my parents and the rest of my family, so I went to a dealership by myself to see what was out there. A salesperson approached me and asked me how much I wanted to spend.

"I don't know," I answered. "I don't even know how much a car costs."

Instead of understanding how early I was in my buying cycle and adjusting to my needs, the salesperson continued to pepper me with questions I couldn't answer. He did nothing to help educate me on the purchase, and then I found myself sitting in his office while he tried to negotiate the price. As you can imagine, I just gave him a blank stare and left.

A rock star salesperson would have assessed where I was in the process and educated me on buying a car. He or she would have understood that rushing the process would only alienate me, but helping me through it could win them a loyal customer for life. Instead, I left and bought my car elsewhere from a competitor.

They apply the right amount of time each week to the right parts of the sale. Many salespeople find it challenging to work on all stages of business development at once. They may work on getting in the door for a while, then work on submitting proposals, and then work on following up and closing. Once deals are in process, too many sellers are tempted (and sometimes encouraged by management) to spend all their time closing. Unfortunately, by the time their deals close, they have nothing in the pipeline and have to start all over again. This causes a delay in new sales and unnecessary peaks and valleys in the sales process. Rock star sellers know how to keep the pipeline flowing smoothly by cultivating prospects at all stages simultaneously. They know that the prospects in the early stage of the pipeline are just as important as the ones in the later stages.

Some salespeople are better at certain stages of the pipeline than others, so they focus on their areas of comfort to the detriment of everything else. Others could be great at every aspect of the sales process, but they don't get results because they just don't put in enough time overall. Rock star sellers know how much time they need to put in to get the outcomes they want, and they distribute that time appropriately over all phases of the sale.

Their lead-nurturing activities actually nurture leads. Any salesperson can look busy all day, but rock star sellers' activities are validated by the results they obtain. They have learned how to nurture their leads effectively, and they don't waste time on activities that don't accomplish that goal. They don't send quick emails that say, "checking in to see if you have any needs"; they instead nominate their prospects for a highly coveted award or invite them to spend time together at an industry-exclusive event. They know that nurturing activities like that create sticky relationships that lead to higher close ratios.

They close sales that are the right size and deliver the right margins. Not all closed sales are created equally. Five closed sales with small profit margins could be less valuable than one closed sale with the right margin. In the same way, large sales with small margins could be less beneficial to the company than smaller sales with larger margins. Rock star sellers understand this and have the patience and perseverance to deliver sales that are the right size with the right margins.

They require very little management supervision because they are self-motivated. Rock star sellers come with their own instincts and their own inner fire. They are intuitive and can feel their way around conversations. You don't have to remind them to stay on task, make that call, or send that email, because they're already on top of it. They won't slack off or procrastinate, because they are self-motivated and want to get the job done.

Most of the time, rock stars know exactly what to do. When they don't, they will ask for help and support. And because they value being able to sell more in less time, they will also be open to new ideas and instruction when you offer it.

Prospects like them, trust them, and want to work with them. There can be a fine line between being patiently persistent and being pushy, but rock star sellers are careful not to cross it. Pushy salespeople are aggressive and obnoxious. They often make it obvious that they care about themselves more than their prospects' needs, so they'll push to close a sale right away to the detriment of the long-term relationship.

Rock star sellers understand that when you're doing business development right, you are building relationships that are valuable not just to your company but to your prospects as well. They understand that the potential for referrals and increasing share of sale can make small deals grow larger over time. They keep the relationship moving forward, but they never rush. They are persistent enough to follow up when they should but patient enough to let a relationship percolate when it needs to.

CARL'S COMMENTS:

Never underestimate the power of a person your customer likes to work with. My company once worked with an IT support firm overseas, and we discovered something fascinating. Some of their most competent technicians—the ones with the highest percentage of error-free work and fewest callbacks—were despised by the customers. Some of the customers went so far as to threaten to take their business elsewhere if the technicians in question were dispatched to them. Many of the more personable technicians had a much worse track record with errors and callbacks, but customers loved them and requested them repeatedly.

They make buying easy for the prospect. Rock star sellers make buying an enjoyable process for the prospect. That's why if company A employs rock star sellers, it will have a decided advantage over company B, which doesn't, even if company A's product or service is inferior to company B's. In the same way, you could have a customer who really wants what you're selling, but if the process is too long or complicated, he or she will delay the purchase or not buy at all.

CARL'S COMMENTS:

My family and I love to go the movies. And for months, every time we would go the employees would ask me, "Would you like to get our ambassador card? All you have to do is go online, click the survey, and fill it out." That always sounded like way too much work for my night off. Then one evening, the woman serving us our popcorn asked us if we wanted to put the purchase on our ambassador card. I explained that we didn't have one and that it always sounded inconvenient to sign up.

"What if I handle the whole thing and you have it in 30 seconds?" She asked. I agreed, she filled out everything for us, and we got our card. She made the process easy and fun, and now I carry the card everywhere. But before that night, you couldn't have paid me to take the darned thing.

DON'T DERAIL YOUR ROCK STARS

When you've got rock star sellers, the last thing you want to do is inadvertently make their jobs more difficult. Fortunately, there are several practical steps you can take to ensure they stay happy and productive.

Have the Right Compensation Plan

Even the best seller can be derailed by the wrong incentives. As we pointed out in the last chapter, salespeople behave the way they get paid. If they're being paid to close the sale by the end of a quarter you may see sellers force a close just to reach the goal, even if taking a little more time might result in a better long-term outcome for the company. If the compensation plan rewards quicker closes over better margins or larger total sales, then you will see sellers adjust their behavior accordingly.

Ideally your plan should not only incentivize the right sales but also discourage the wrong sales. For example, if a sale closes quickly but it's not as profitable as it could have been, that should be reflected in the seller's commission or at least in the performance review. Sales goals can also be refined so that a sale below a certain margin level will be ineligible for any additional rewards or bonuses you offer.

The car dealership I visited in my 20s almost certainly had a simple incentive structure that rewarded salespeople for getting cars off the lot quickly. That's why it's often a good idea to reward sellers not just for the close but also for the major events that should lead up to it. In many industries, producing a certain number of meetings will produce a certain number of proposals, which in turn will produce a certain number of closes. You can reward sellers for meetings, as long as you're very clear about what constitutes a meeting that earns a reward. You can also offer rewards for having a certain number of proposals in the pipeline, as long as you offer similarly clear parameters.

These kinds of incentives will encourage your sellers to stay on track and work toward the results you want; they'll also ensure that rock star sellers feel valued and appreciated. The rewards do not have to be large cash bonuses; they just have to be meaningful to the people receiving them. I had a colleague years ago who was one of the top salespeople in our company, but he had a tiny office. I asked him why this was the case, and he explained that he preferred the reward in his check rather than in the square footage of his workspace. Someone else might have felt differently, but the important thing was the company responded to how the seller wanted to be rewarded.

Another VP of sales I know keeps a jar on her desk filled with gift cards to anywhere from Home Depot to Starbucks to some local spas. When salespeople hit particular milestones, they get to pick out the gift card that they prefer. Sometimes balloons, an Employee of the Week program, or just buying pizza for the team at the end of a week when they've hit their targets is enough to make everyone feel appreciated and encouraged.

The right incentives can also help salespeople stay on top of the tasks they enjoy the least. For example, you can make certain rewards contingent on getting their expense reports done on time, attending 90 percent of the sales meetings, or having all their contracts properly signed and dated. Ultimately you want your sellers to work to win at the game according to the rules you've set. Make sure the rules are clear and lead to the behaviors and the results that you want.

CARL'S COMMENTS:

Real rock stars—the musicians—aren't perfect. They give amazing concerts, but they may also trash a hotel room now and then. Rock star sellers aren't perfect either. When my salespeople call into the office, they're often a little abrupt. The administrative team is not always thrilled with them. But they're driven, they're focused, and they're getting the job done. While you need to set basic boundaries that define acceptable behavior, you've also got to give your rock stars room to be human.

Minimize Non-Sales Activities by Providing the Right Support

Although a certain amount of paperwork is unavoidable, rock star sellers function best when they are totally focused on selling. In fact, many will resent any activities that don't directly lead to new dollars and view them as a waste of time. Business owners can support rock star sellers by making sure that their administrative tasks are not excessively time consuming. There are many ways to do this:

1. **Support their use of the CRM.** As important as CRMs are to management and sales staff, a lot of companies have trouble getting their sellers to enter all the information they should on a consistent and timely basis. Most CRMs require you to click three times to get to the notes section and then three times to get out. This can seem intolerably slow to someone with a list of prospects to call or meet.

   One solution is to allow sellers to type their notes into an email to the support staff member, who can then enter them into the CRM. This saves the sellers time and allows them to record the information while it's fresh in their minds, without disrupting the flow of their day. There are also voice systems where sellers can audio record their notes to be entered electronically or by a support person. For an article on CRM best practices, go to www.BizDevDoneRightBook/crmbestpractices.com

2. **Support the sellers' written correspondence.** At various stages of the sale, support staff can provide templates of certain emails based on the company's sales messaging. This allows the seller to spend just a couple minutes customizing the email, rather than having to generate it from scratch. It takes significantly less time to edit than to craft.

3. **Support sellers while they're in the car.** Many salespeople spend a lot of time driving from one appointment to the next, preventing them from being able to type or text. A support person can take dictated emails or notes and make that drive time much more productive, allowing salespeople to nurture relationships while they're away from their desks.

Once you've gone to all the trouble to find and hire a rock star seller, don't skimp on the administrative support to keep that seller productive. Fortunately, most administrative support is quite affordable. Even on a tight budget, you can use a combination of interns, virtual assistants, outsourcing, and talk-to-text technology to keep your sellers from getting mired in administrative work.

Now you know how to identify the rock stars on your sales staff and how to reward them, support them, and keep them selling for you. But what about their ongoing training? We'll cover that in the next chapter.

CHAPTER 8

WHO IS RESPON- SIBLE for TED*UCATION?*

*– Tailored Training, Education &
Demonstration of Proficiency*

TEDUCATION

N ow that you've learned how to recognize a rock star seller, you may feel like firing your entire sales team and starting over. But most of us can't do that. Instead, we need to get the most out of what we have right now.

That's where TEDUCATION comes in. TEDUCATION is the key to ensuring that you maximize the talent and abilities of your sales team from the very start. It will keep your rock star sellers at the top of their game and help your not-so-rock star sellers improve. TEDUCATION is Tailored Training, Education, and Demonstrating Proficiency, and it offers you the quickest path to business development done right.

In this chapter, you'll get up close and personal with TEDUCATION and how it can maximize your team's productivity. Standardized sales training is very important, but performance can't be optimal without TEDUCATION. Even if you've got a seller who is struggling, give TEDUCATION the opportunity to turn that seller's performance around.

TAILORED TRAINING

Tailored training for sales is the customized guidance and tools that individual sellers need in order to accelerate success in their markets and in the sales situations they are most likely to encounter. The tailored training that an individual requires will change over time as he or she continues to grow as a sales professional. Tailored training can mean customizing a particular sales message for a particular situation, and it can also mean customizing the precise teaching for an individual.

Tools for Success from the Start

Tailored training is a vital part of equipping new sellers with the tools they need to be successful. Salespeople who are new to your company will not automatically know the best way in the door with prospects for your sale or which story works best in response to a particular objection. You want new sellers to learn this information right away, so they can become as effective as possible in the shortest amount of time.

Unfortunately, many companies onboard their new sellers by just ordering their business cards and sending them out with a more experienced team member to show them the ropes. They may ride along on a few sales visits or sit with people while they're on the phone. But shadowing a top seller or even the sales manager a couple of times won't necessarily teach a new salesperson how to answer a prospect's specific objection when a $500,000 deal is on the line.

When a sales team isn't performing up to expectations, it's easy to blame the sellers themselves. And maybe not all of them are rock stars. But consider the possibility that the team is underperforming because management hasn't given them the tools they need to succeed.

The good news is that both Carl and I have found that you can grow your business from 10 to 30 percent with the team you have in place if you just give them the right tools and training. Even if you don't have a team of rock stars, you can still help the sellers you have increase their success if you pinpoint their areas of weakness and offer the tailored training they need.

Setting Realistic Benchmarks Helps Identify Training Needs

How do you determine what kind of training your sellers need? Recently I was working with a seller, "Sean," who seemed to be doing everything right but still wasn't hitting the benchmarks we expected. He had a well-researched list of prospects, and he'd demonstrated proficiency in the messaging and the answers for the objections. So to figure out what was going wrong, I sat with him while he was making his prospect calls.

What I learned by listening to Sean was that when the prospect was ready to take the next step, Sean was uncomfortable asking for a date and time to meet. So he would continue speaking about the service, drawing out the conversation with unnecessary information. My tailored training for Sean was to hold up a single sheet of paper with the words "Date and Time" written on it. As he continued to make calls, I held up that paper in front of him and pointed to it repeatedly.

This might seem like an unusual form of training, but by the end of that day, Sean was proficiently asking for the date and time and taking his prospects to the next step. This was a very small point, but making this tailored training adjustment made all the difference in the world. Sometimes the answer to how to increase sales is in the minutia.

The key to effective training is to identify the specific steps of the sales process from initial contact to close, and then set realistic benchmarks for each step. When a team member fails to hit a benchmark, you zero in on that step just like I did with Sean. Then you can pinpoint the problem and tailor the training to what the seller needs.

Setting benchmarks also allows you to pinpoint your sellers' strengths. In some cases, it may make sense to divide the sales process up between different team members. The people who are good at getting in the door can start the process and then hand it off to those who are good at going to the meetings and nurturing leads. Those sellers may even hand the deal off to another team of closers. While this isn't ideal for every situation, it can work great in a family-run business, for example, where there may not be as much flexibility with hiring and firing. Allowing team members to specialize can help you get the most out of everyone, as long as the hand-offs are smooth.

Tailored Training vs. Standardized Training

Once salespeople have been hired and given their initial training, most companies will either cease training them altogether or send them to conferences for general training. This kind of training is important. I know several different companies and individuals who offer it, and they do an excellent job helping sellers to increase their overall proficiency.

But those training programs can't do what I did for Sean: pinpoint a specific individual's weakness and address it directly. Sean didn't need to be told to have more energy and passion in his delivery. He needed to be reminded to ask for a time and date at a specific moment in a prospect conversation. General training can't teach your sellers your sales message or the answer to a company specific objection.

Much of the sales process can be learned and mastered...

...by willing sellers.

So who is responsible for all this tailored training? At the end of the day, the business owners or sales VPs are responsible for making sure it happens. Unfortunately, too often they don't. It's my experience that they either don't think about this kind of training, or they don't know how to provide it. They can hire an outside consultant to help them if they are unsure. Regardless of who actually does the training, the business owner or the sales VP is responsible for identifying what the sellers need to improve and finding a way to give it to them.

EDUCATION

In addition to developing and refining their business development skills, sellers also need to become authorities on the products or services they sell as well as the issues and challenges their decision makers face. They should be able to come across to prospects as experts on the industry itself, so when they present the solution, their recommendation is credible. Offer your staff ongoing education to ensure they obtain and maintain this expertise. Knowledge is always power.

Buyers today are smart. By the time customers come in to purchase an item, whether it's a truck, a computer, or a software package, chances are they've already read a lot about the product. That means that your sellers are not going to impress unless they know significantly more than the buyers do.

When sellers are experts on the technical aspects of the product or service they sell, they are more successful bringing value to prospects at every stage of the sale. The more familiar they are with the nuances of a particular industry, the better they understand which emotional notes to hit in each communication.

Offering continual education will give your sellers a tremendous competitive edge since your competition probably won't bother. Your team can be not only the best-trained sellers out there but also the best educated.

DEMONSTRATING PROFICIENCY

We've repeatedly emphasized the importance of having your sellers demonstrate proficiency with the message and the answers to objections before you unleash them on prospects. But what does this look like in practical terms?

Once you've hired new sellers and given them standardized sales training, tailored training, and education on what they are selling and to whom, you're still not going to send them out into the market quite yet. Instead, you'll have them role play to prove that they're ready to sell. This step doesn't take much time, but you'll reap tremendous benefits from it.

When playing the role of a buyer, you'll first go through basic situations to allow sellers to demonstrate their mastery of the messaging and answers for the typical objections they're likely to encounter. Don't just read from the manual; insert each objection into a sales scenario that might actually happen. You're not only looking for proficiency in delivering the answer but also in discerning which objection you're facing in the first place. The objection you hear is not always the objection you're facing.

You'll want to act out realistic scenarios from each stage of the sale and listen for the sellers' ability to ask questions that will allow them to customize the message further. Finally, your sellers should demonstrate the ability to bring the conversation to that Moment of Yes®, where prospects see your company as exactly the right solution.

You also want to use the opportunity to throw them a few curve balls. One of my favorites is to have the person playing the buyer say to the seller, "Thank you for coming. Listen, my boss just called me into a meeting. I know I said we'd have an hour, but I'm going to need you to keep it under five minutes. Go ahead."

At that point the seller must be able to determine how to make the most of those five minutes. A typical response might be to try to cram an entire presentation into a couple minutes by speed talking and skipping over important information. Rather, the seller should say something like: "Five minutes. Okay. Let's hit just a few key points. But before we do that let's set a date to get together when you have more time. How is Thursday at 10:00 a.m. for you?" Then it's time to take out the calendars to ensure that the next step is secured before the five minutes are up.

These role playing exercises will not only help you gauge what additional practice your sellers need, they will also give them added confidence. The more they practice with different scenarios, the better they'll be able to improvise when confronted with something for which they weren't specifically prepared.

Giving your sellers the opportunity to demonstrate proficiency shouldn't be a one-time activity. You can go through these exercises briefly once a quarter, which will let you know exactly where problems lie. Think of it like a regular checkup that helps you ensure that your sellers stay at the top of their game. For tips on demonstrating messaging proficiency, go to www.BizDevDoneRightBook.com/messagingproficiency.com

Scoring Proficiency

Keep in mind that you and your sellers may have very different perceptions of their performance in these role playing exercises. Rather than just offering general feedback, score them on a scale of 1 to 10 for each skill you want to see. This will help them know exactly where they stand: what they're doing well and what they need to improve. Looking at the numbers will let you know how to tailor the training and whether you need to coach them up or coach them out. (We'll cover that decision in more detail in the next chapter.)

Generally speaking, you want your team members at an 8 or above in every area. Realistically, some may be outstanding—a 9 or a 10—in some skills and never quite get to that 8 in another. Others will likely have one or two very low areas, particularly when they first start. In those cases, you can have that seller take a secondary role in weak activities while they receive tailored training. That could be direct coaching from you, or they could shadow a partner or manager who is strong in that area. This allows you to get the most out of the salesperson without jeopardizing a major part of the sales process by sending someone out there who isn't up to the job.

Offering your sellers regular opportunities to demonstrate proficiency means that you'll never have an issue that goes unchecked for months at a time. It allows you to offer further tailored training and education to get the most out of the team you've got, and it will help you make the right personnel decisions when necessary.

TRUST TEDUCATION

Tailored training, ongoing education, and continual demonstration of proficiency give your sellers the tools they need to be successful. TEDUCATION will tell you what you've got and how to make the most of it, as well as how to onboard new sellers in a way that positions them for success in the shortest possible time. TEDUCATION allows all your sellers to know where they stand and what they need to improve. And you can see a 10 to 30 percent increase in your business just by putting TEDUCATION to work in your company right now.

CHAPTER 9

COACH 'EM UP or COACH 'EM OUT!

– How To Know When it's Time to Give Up.

COACH 'EM UP OR
COACH 'EM OUT

M any experts urge business owners to "hire slowly and fire quickly," but this can actually be a recipe for tremendous frustration and financial loss. In this chapter, you'll learn why Carl and I advise our respective clients instead **to hire slowly and fire strategically.**

The hire slowly, fire quickly mantra arose in response to the fact that too many hire quickly and fire slowly. And it's true that most business owners hire sellers without going through the process we described in chapter 6 and then may allow a bad hire to hang around too long, wasting money and opportunities.

Hire slowly...

...fire strategically.

But just as it can be expensive to wait too long to fire, it can also be expensive to fire too quickly. Before you actually let a salesperson go, take the time to be sure that individual is really the problem. Then you can fire when the decision serves your strategic interests.

In this chapter, you will learn how to diagnose the exact cause behind performance issues, as well as how to analyze the costs and benefits of firing sales staff. Then you'll be able to decide whether it's best to coach them up or coach them out.

THE PERILS OF FIRING TOO QUICKLY

While you certainly don't want to let the wrong seller hang around too long, firing underperforming sellers quickly is not necessarily the best decision. It is often much cheaper and better for the company to provide additional training to the sellers you have or to make needed adjustments to your sales process or to the job responsibilities within your sales organization. These kinds of changes often improve performance without the costs of firing and rehiring.

Unfortunately, many business owners become frustrated with a seller's results and assume firing and rehiring will automatically improve the bottom line. Firing a seller is the right move when you are 100 percent certain that the root of the problem lies with the person himself or herself and not with any other factors. Unless you are sure this is the case, you run the risk of treating only the symptoms instead of the problem itself.

If the cause of underperformance lies with the sales process, unrealistic expectations, or a failure to give sellers adequate tools to do their jobs well, you can hire a new person, but you'll still have exactly the same issues six months down the road. If the problem is caused by something minor that the seller can learn to do differently, firing means you will have wasted a great deal of money for something that could have been fixed relatively easily. If the problem is the result of the seller being great in some aspects of sales and weak in others, then firing means you lose the talent the seller had in those areas.

When you fire business development professionals, you are not only giving up all the training and salary you invested in them; you may also lose the contacts they were developing. You are potentially sacrificing a pipeline of relationships they were cultivating: hours of conversations and possibly even proposals they have in the market.

This loss is even more pronounced in industries with longer sales cycles. Some media companies, for example, have a two-year sales cycle. If they fire a seller after a year and half, the company may lose several deals that would have closed had they waited just a few months longer. On top of this, they have the added cost of recruiting and training a replacement.

None of this means you should never fire; it just means you should consider the decision carefully. Take the extra time to properly diagnose the problem with the seller's performance and do everything possible to rectify the situation.

DIAGNOSE THE PROBLEM ACCURATELY

An accurate diagnosis begins with asking the right questions. Why are you not seeing the results you were hoping for from the salesperson? Does the salesperson have all the tools he or she needs to do the job well? Are the expectations realistic and benchmarks designed to give the right information? And if the salesperson is doing something wrong, can it be fixed?

To find the "something" that the salesperson may be doing wrong, my company will create a flowchart for the entire sales process for our clients. It will begin with how the prospect list is researched and created, cover every single contact and touch point, and end with the close. Like a doctor looking at blood work and X-rays, we examine the execution of every step in great detail until we uncover the ones that are not going as they should.

We had a client company that was ready to fire its entire sales staff. They called us in to help them make the final decision. We did this analysis and uncovered three steps in the sales process where the staff wasn't executing correctly. The first was a particular objection that none of the sellers could answer. The second was a failure to get to the next step with prospects after submitting a proposal. Third, the sellers were not tailoring their proposals to the prospect's specific needs. Interestingly, all the sellers were having the same issues, suggesting that the problem lay not with the sellers themselves but with the process and tools they were given.

Fortunately, all of these problems were fixable. For the first item, we had management create the right language to answer the objection and train the sales staff in the delivery of that answer. For the second, we had the salespeople ask the prospect for a date and time to review the proposal when the proposal request was initially made. Third, we provided "high gain" questions for sellers to ask at the time the prospect asked for the proposal, which would help personalize it.

Before this intervention, the sellers were submitting book-length proposals and the prospects were setting them aside to review "later." Too often later never came. The questions we had the sellers ask allowed them to structure the proposals in a streamlined way that ensured they were not set aside and were a slam dunk against what the prospects were looking for.

If this company had responded to their disappointing sales by firing their sellers and rehiring, they still would likely have faced exactly the same problems with the new sellers. Taking the time to diagnose the problem systematically saved them a lot of money that would have been spent recruiting, training, and making up for large gaps in the pipeline. For more information on how to diagnose the right sales problem, go to www.BizDevDoneRightBook.com/fix-therightproblem.com

CARL'S COMMENTS:

One of my clients runs a membership-based business, and one of the cofounders likes to inform everyone that she is not a salesperson. When she would go to networking meetings and not get results, she would just repeat her conviction that she was not a salesperson.

We analyzed their sales process and found it consisted of five major steps. They met the prospects, followed up, invited them to their facility for an assessment, presented a proposal, and then closed. The cofounder was only struggling with one step: she couldn't seem to get prospects to come in to take the assessment. She thought the entire process was a failure, when in fact she was actually doing a great job with the earlier part of the pipeline.

When we interviewed the people that she had met up to that point, we found that they all loved her. But she never really gave them a clear call to action regarding the meeting and assessment. She would say something vague, asking them to come by when they had a chance, rather than setting a concrete date and time. We made that small adjustment, and this "non-salesperson" saw her results improve dramatically.

Both these stories demonstrate how a small adjustment in the sales process can make a huge difference in results but only if you know which adjustment to make. I was giving a seminar one day and a young woman in the audience was having trouble getting initial meetings. After I asked her a few questions, it became obvious she was hiding behind email and not also using live calls to secure her meetings. The voice-email combination is a very powerful way to initiate relationships. Success is significantly less likely without both. But many younger sellers are more comfortable with email and texting than they are with calling. I was able to explain to her how to make this simple adjustment that she wouldn't have known to make otherwise.

Sometimes the problem is in the minutia or is so subtle or out of the ordinary that you have to observe the seller directly to determine what it is. With one of my clients, we discovered that a seller was not securing the number of meetings his managers expected because he always did his calls to California prospects on Thursdays, even when those decision makers requested he call them at the beginning of the week. Strange, I know, but you can't make this stuff up! This was an unusual problem but very fixable. Imagine how stunned his manager was to learn that this was going on.

The problem you can never fix is the one you don't know about. Often underperforming sellers are just the messengers of a problem, not the problem itself. It is expensive and unfair to terminate an employee who may simply be following a flawed procedure or struggling with inadequate tools for the job. If you're not satisfied with your sales results, take the time to investigate and properly diagnose what's going on. You'll save yourself and everyone else a lot of time and money.

Engage an Expert

Many business development managers or sales VPs entered into those management roles because they were stellar salespeople, not because they had years of experience diagnosing systemic sales problems. Sometimes it takes an experienced and emotionally neutral third party expert to assess the problem correctly and determine whether it is fixable or not. After years of mapping out sales processes, it's easy for effective consultants to figure out what's going on and offer a comprehensive analysis of the costs and benefits of keeping or firing a particular seller. Just like an experienced doctor can diagnose the root cause of a problem and make adjustments that would prevent a costly and painful surgery, Carl and I have saved many companies from making the wrong personnel decisions.

For example, I was hired by a business owner to evaluate a salesperson who wasn't closing the number of deals the owner expected. He was getting plenty of meetings, and everything he reported back to us about those meetings sounded great. So we finally went with him to some of the meetings to observe him. We found that he did many things right: he structured the meeting correctly and asked great questions. But when the prospects answered his questions, he was not able to identify the opportunities within the dialogue and formulate a response that moved the conversation forward. He should have been able to incorporate the prospects' explanations of their specific concerns and challenges into his answers and present his company as exactly the right solution. Instead, he appeared to listen but then went through the standard capability presentation from start to finish the same way every time, regardless of the information the prospect had shared.

The salesperson was still able to get to a follow-up next step with these prospects, but the next step was not what it would have been had the discussion focused on the opportunity versus the canned presentation. This caused the company to miss out on too many opportunities and explained why the seller wasn't closing enough deals. This was not just a listening problem; it was a problem with knowing what to listen for and how to act on it. Because of my years of experience, I was able to determine that it wasn't worth the investment for the company to fix the issue with the seller. It was more beneficial in this situation to fire and start with a new seller who possessed these skills from the start. In this case, the amount of time it would have taken to make this individual proficient in this critical part of the sales process was not worth it for my client. There is no way the owner would have known this seller's exact problem without directly observing him.

Examine Work Ethic and Attitude

All sellers are in control of the attitude they bring to work and the effort they apply all day. As a boss, you can't fix someone who comes to work with a bad attitude or someone who is simply lazy. But sometimes what looks like an issue with work ethic is actually a little more complicated.

Being lazy is not quite the same as being reluctant or uncomfortable with certain tasks. Depending on your situation, these can be problems you manage rather than solve. One business owner Carl and I know hired a new salesperson, only to discover six months later that the seller wasn't comfortable opening new doors. He was, however, very good at developing relationships once he was in the meeting and then bringing those relationships to closed sales. In this case the best way to manage the situation was to split the sales function and assign the door-opening responsibilities to someone else.

Most people do not come to work determined to do a bad job, but realistically, no salesperson is perfect at every step of the sales process. The real question is whether or not they have a good attitude and are willing to learn. Will they accept coaching and constructive criticism? Are they willing to work at improving the areas where they're not strong enough? Is the problem fixable by reallocating the tasks within the sales process or by altering the process itself? If they are, the seller is likely salvageable, at least until you can find a better option.

Map Out the Business Process

We've already discussed the benefits of documenting every step of your sales process from initial contact to close. But it is also very important to map out your entire business process—from sales to billing and fulfillment—to pinpoint any places where your sellers may be getting entangled in non-sales activities.

Effective sellers should be empowered to spend as much of their time as possible on business development, not on non-sales activities. Yet various circumstances cause salespeople to become involved in customer service, strategic planning, report generation, and other activities that don't directly generate new dollars. **Remember, every time managers ask sellers to spend time on non-revenue-generating work, they are not generating revenue.** This may seem like a simple concept, but we see too many inefficiencies here. If your goal is more sales, think twice about how your sellers spend their time.

CARL'S COMMENTS:

I recently had a situation with a client company where the sellers were getting involved with non-sales activities. The boss wasn't asking them to do anything outside their sales duties, but they were choosing to spend their time that way. The sellers were submitting their orders to product fulfillment, but the products weren't getting to their customers fast enough. So the customers were getting upset and calling the sellers. The sellers investigated and found out there were all sorts of issues in the product fulfillment department.

In an effort to make sure their customers were properly taken care of, the sellers got mired in all sorts of work that they shouldn't have been doing. In the end, when my company was able to diagnose the problem correctly, the business owner cleaned house in his product fulfillment department and put his sellers back to work making sales.

As Carl's story illustrates, problems can arise when there is inadequate communication between sales and other departments. I was brought in to assess a situation with a seller, "Jason," who was very capable but wasn't producing what his boss expected. I asked Jason a series of questions, starting with: "What is preventing you from selling more?"

"I need more time," he answered.

"Why don't you have more time?" I asked.

"Because I'm constantly dealing with customers," he explained.

Now, Jason's boss had set up a very logical procedure where the operations people were assigned to handle any incoming customer service calls. The problem was that Jason wasn't confident that the operations person assigned to his customers—"Sarah"—was going to handle issues in a time frame that he felt was acceptable. Jason, in his desire to help his customers, decided that he would take those calls, because his response time was faster.

The solution was to get Jason and Sarah together for a detailed conversation. Sarah needed to understand what Jason considered an acceptable time frame for handling an issue, and Jason needed to understand different factors that might prevent Sarah from being able to handle the issue in a timely manner.

Based on what they communicated in the meeting, we were able to come to a resolution, and Jason was able to get back to selling. When you can map out each stage of your business process from sale to fulfillment, it's much easier to pinpoint any gaps and ensure that you're maximizing your sellers' time.

Personal Issues

Your sellers' scorecards don't lie, but they don't always tell the whole story. Sometimes sellers are underperforming because of personal issues. Divorce, relationship problems, caring for a sick loved one, or even substance abuse or dependency are just a few of the "behind the scenes" factors that could be affecting someone's job performance. As with any other performance issue, the first step is to diagnose the problem correctly and then determine whether the person is willing to work through the problem.

CALCULATE THE COST

Even if you've concluded a seller's deficiencies aren't fixable, you need to calculate what firing a seller will actually cost you. My company has one client who wanted her salesperson to make 50 meetings in one year. At the end of the year, the salesperson had made 43. The owner considered this result a failure and contemplated firing the seller. Although the seller failed to meet the benchmark, was getting rid of him worth throwing away the potential of another 43 meetings next year? Here are three measures you may want to consider before you fire:

Revenue per Appointment

If you want to understand the financial impact of hiring and starting again, examine your sellers' revenue per appointment. You can calculate this easily by taking the sales they generated and dividing that by the number of appointments they went out on. This will give you a good picture of how much money they are bringing to the company. Use this metric after a seller has gone through at least one sales cycle. Don't be too quick to fire people who are making money for you, especially if you don't have other people who are already generating the revenue you will lose when you fire.

Close Ratio

Your sellers' close ratio is simply how many times they come back with a deal compared to how many times you send them out. How well are they converting the leads your company is generating? How many opportunities would you miss out on if you let them go? Again, use this metric *after* a seller has gone through at least one sales cycle.

These two numbers will give you a quick analysis of the immediate financial impact of the fire. Even if you bring in someone new tomorrow, he or she is not going to be able to produce immediately. The ramp-up time for a new salesperson is usually the length of the sales cycle plus additional time for training and adjustment. This can be six months to a year or even more, depending on your industry.

RSROI (Rock Star Return on Investment)

A critical measure to review before firing is whether the seller is paying for himself with the sales he's bringing in. To calculate this, add all the costs for your seller including salary, incentives, and benefits, as well as all other soft costs. Then compare that with the gross margin from the sales he's brought in after one complete sales cycle. Is he paying for himself?

TIMING IS EVERYTHING

Just because you decide you need to fire a salesperson does not mean you need to do it immediately. This leaves an opening in your sales staff until you bring in someone new. Instead, you can actually hire someone new and fire after the new person is up and running. As long as the people you're letting go are covering their costs, there is really no downside to keeping them until your new sellers are trained, acclimated, and generating enough revenue to prove they're better than what you have.

Managing the transition after the fire is critical to avoiding the loss of any progress that the previous seller made with various prospects. Here are a few tips to make any transition a smooth one:

Have Good Records

Make sure your policies require your sellers to keep good notes. Whatever CRM system you use, sellers should keep detailed records, including contact information and the history of all the salesperson's interactions with each prospect. This is also important for illness or emergencies.

Ensure Relationship Continuity

Someone in the company besides the seller should also have a relationship with the key decision makers at your prospect and client companies. This way if the seller leaves for any reason, you have someone else in the organization who can step in and have continuity with the prospects and clients. Sellers can also exit your company voluntarily at any time. Having more than one person develop a relationship with key prospects and clients is your insurance policy.

Consider Having the Departing Seller Help with the Transition

Depending on circumstances surrounding the fire, you might want to provide an incentive for the departing seller to assist with the transition. This assistance could include making a round of phone calls or setting up a round of meetings to introduce the new person. The incentive you offer will likely be worth a fraction of the value of keeping continuity in those relationships.

So now you understand that giving up too soon is expensive, but so is giving up too late. You know the basics of pinpointing the problem, determining if it lies with the seller and whether or not it is fixable. If you don't feel confident diagnosing the problem or determining whether it's fixable on your own, you can bring in an outside expert to help.

The best decision for your company isn't always the easiest one. But the best decision will minimize your costs while getting the most out of what you already have.

CHAPTER 10

THERE'S NO CHEESE DOWN THAT TUNNEL!

– Avoiding the "Shiny Object" Syndrome.

THERE'S NO CHEESE DOWN THAT TUNNEL!

E ven with a team of rock star sellers, it can be very tricky to figure out the exact recipe for business development that works for your company. In fact, many business owners never really discover their winning formula. Instead, some get stuck in a rut, doing the same things over and over again, hoping for different results. Others are like mice running around in a maze, racing down tunnel after tunnel, looking for cheese that always seems to elude them.

The world seems to offer every kind of business development program imaginable, so how do you know which ones will get the job done for your company? This chapter will teach you a simple process to evaluate any business development initiative objectively, whether it's something you've been doing for years or a brand new program that was just brought to your attention. You'll learn to sniff out the tunnels where the cheese is hiding and avoid the ones that lead to dead ends.

IDENTIFY WHAT YOU REALLY WANT

In any given month, you'll be confronted with dozens of opportunities to initiate marketing campaigns—direct mail, SEO, pay-per-click, and so on—as well as to attend networking events or trade shows. Before you evaluate any program or initiative, take the time to determine what you really want to get out of it.

I worked with a company that routinely invested six figures into several trade shows over the course of a year. Then we sat down and talked about what they really wanted out of their business development efforts. Their top priority was securing initial meetings with qualified high-level decision makers, but it turned out that virtually none of their target prospects attended these trade shows. Their underlings were there, but the executives were not. The events were a lot of fun and had become part of their corporate culture, but they weren't really producing what the owners were looking for. They weren't a direct path to starting conversations and relationships with exactly the right prospects, because those people didn't attend.

Often business development professionals and their managers become emotionally attached to certain programs and lose the ability to evaluate them objectively. Trade shows may be great for creating brand awareness but not necessarily as effective for getting meetings with high-level decision makers. If you want the inside secret for mastering trade show effectiveness, go to www.BizDevDoneRight-Book.com\tradeshoweffectiveness.com

FIVE STEPS TO EVALUATING A BUSINESS DEVELOPMENT INITIATIVE

Deciding which business development programs to implement doesn't need to be complicated or confusing. If you approach the process systematically, the decision can be simple and straightforward. Here are five steps we've developed to evaluate any initiative you're considering:

Step 1:
Gather Historical Data

The first step in evaluating a program effectively is to investigate past results. This was easy to do in the case of the company that went to so many trade shows every year. We simply had to calculate how many qualified leads led to a meeting, an order, or a proposal, since that was their goal. It is a good idea to regularly evaluate your current business development initiatives to ensure they are still delivering intended outcomes.

If you're considering a program that you haven't used before, find some business owners or sales VPs who have used it and ask them what their results were. Ideally, you want to gather data from as many people as possible, spanning multiple years of participation. What results have they seen each year? If some of them no longer attend the event or use the program, find out why. They may not have found it effective, or their needs or goals may have changed. Whether their responses are positive or negative, you will gain a lot of useful information from asking these questions.

Step 2:
Assess the Probability of Success and Develop a Timeline

Once you've gathered data for the program, you are ready to assess the likelihood that the investment of time and money will be worthwhile. Based on your company's capabilities and the experiences others have had, what is the probability that your participation will produce the desired results? If it sounds like you'll either break even or make money, there is little downside in giving the program a try. If you feel there is significant upside potential, then not trying the program would be foolish.

As you're making this assessment, you want to develop a timeline for what success looks like at each stage of the program. When we speak with our clients about our Door Opener® Service, we work with them to develop a clear timeline for when they can expect new meetings, new orders from these meetings, cash from those orders, and most importantly, ROI. This timeline defines a successful program based on your specific company and industry and allows you to evaluate whether the program is delivering according to plan.

Step 3:
Anticipate What Would Prevent Success

After you've assessed the probability of success, it's important to think of anything that could go wrong. You want to outline your worst-case scenarios and then create a plan to hedge against them. Sometimes Mother Nature ruins outdoor events and causes indoor events to be poorly attended. If you're doing a series of interviews on television and radio, there is always the possibility you'll be preempted for bigger news. There's a potential downside to every program, but thinking about it ahead of time can help you mitigate those risks. Then you can develop a contingency plan for everything that could go wrong.

CARL'S COMMENTS:

My company attended a trade show in the middle of winter, and Mother Nature showed up on opening day with subzero temperatures, snow, and ice. Fortunately, we had planned for this possibility, and we weren't relying solely on the outside attendees to make this event successful for us. In anticipation of possible bad weather, we had targeted exhibitors as well as public traffic. We emailed all the exhibitors in advance, scheduling a number of one-to-one meetings. Even though we would have preferred good weather, the trade show turned out to be very productive for us.

Step 4:
Solicit Expert Input

Your next step is to solicit input on the program from subject matter experts. These are people who will be brutally honest with you. They have no dog in the fight, and they're not worried about hurting your feelings. Listen to what they say, and consider their opinions, guidance, and experiences seriously.

Some business owners will ask their friends for feedback, which is understandable. However, if those friends don't have experience or expertise with what you're trying to accomplish, they may agree with your plans simply to make you feel good. Other acquaintances may offer criticism just to appear smart or authoritative.

Make sure to ask your experts good questions. Ask them if they see any holes in your plan: something you haven't anticipated or accounted for. Ask them about any experiences they have with similar plans and what approach they would take if they were in your situation. Importantly, ask them how to mitigate potential risk with the program you're considering.

Now, the advice you'll get in response to these kinds of questions will not be irrefutable wisdom from on high, but it will give you a better picture of the possible downsides you hadn't considered before. Sometimes you may want to reconsider the whole plan based on their advice, but more than likely you'll just make a couple of adjustments before moving forward.

Step 5:
Compare Your Results to the Projections

When it comes time to pull the trigger on a new business development initiative, some business owners will allow fear to get the better of them. They will repeat steps 2 through 4 over and over, delaying the start indefinitely. But once you've gathered historical data, calculated your probability of success, anticipated any obstacles, and solicited input, take the plunge and get going. Jump in with both feet and keep looking forward. Never forget that there is also a cost to doing nothing.

As soon as you've implemented the plan, compare the results to your initial projections. This will show you if the plan is delivering (or on track to deliver) what you expected. IMPORTANT: Be sure you're evaluating everything according to the timeline you set up in step 2. If you do this from the very beginning, you'll have an early warning if things aren't going the way they should, enabling you to make course corrections when necessary.

The popular book, *What to Expect When You're Expecting*, helps new mothers know what changes they're likely to experience in each stage of pregnancy. In the same spirit, my company put together a document that explains what to expect during the first 16 weeks after you go live with our Door Opener® Service. We offer descriptions and metrics for each phase, which allows our clients to monitor the program to ensure it's on track. Of course, we monitor the results as well and make adjustments if something isn't working the way it should. By the time we get to 16 weeks, all those little course corrections ensure we are on or ahead of schedule.

If you're using an outside vendor for your program, ask him to prepare a document like this. If it's an internal initiative, ask one of your salespeople to create it. Of course, the delivery for every industry and every company is going to be different, but there should be benchmarks and measurements that you can realistically expect to hit. Evaluating progress according to the timeline ensures that you don't pull the plug before the final results are in.

REMAIN EMOTIONALLY NEUTRAL

The purpose of this five-step process is to enable you to detach yourself from the programs you're considering and evaluate them objectively. Just like a fondness for a particular company could cloud your judgment when you're buying or selling a stock, an attachment to an event or a project can make it difficult to gauge its true effectiveness. Conversely, bad experiences can cause you to resist a new program irrationally or make you overly hesitant to start.

Toxic Hesitation

A certain degree of caution is always a good idea, but too much hesitation can lead to very bad decisions. It's much better to go "all in" with a program you are confident can work, rather than to build incrementally with programs that are likely to fail. We were talking with a company that needed to get in the door with high-level executives and loved the idea of our Door Opener® Service, but the owner couldn't bring himself to make the investment. Instead, they hired a very low-level telemarketing company. The junior sellers might have been strong in selling coffee to an office manager but could not hold a conversation with a senior executive that produced a result. That program cost less but produced absolutely nothing: most of the time they didn't get in the door, and the meetings they did get weren't worth having. The owner spent some more money and hired a salesperson. But that seller didn't know how to open doors either, so six months later the company fired him. And then they came back to us to do it right.

Once you've done your due diligence by going through the five steps we've listed, move forward with confidence. Don't let fear prevent you from doing something right.

Don't Second-Guess Success

There will always be opportunities to doubt your decisions, but if a program is producing the desired results, don't waste time or energy second guessing your success. Likewise, if a program is successfully paying for itself, don't replace it with a program that has the possibility of delivering better results. Instead, add the second program to what you are already doing. Then once both are running well you can decide whether you want to replace one with the other or keep them both going, further mitigating risk.

CARL'S COMMENTS:

When I wrote *The 7 Stages of Small-Business Success*, I interviewed people about a potential real estate deal. I asked them to pretend they were selling a piece of land. They had done all their research, consulted experts, and decided on a price of $100,000. Then I asked, "If on the first day the land goes on the market, the first person who looks at it buys it at full price with no questions asked, did you ask the right price?"

A lot of them weren't sure. They know if the land sits around on the market for six months the price was wrong, but they're not sure if the price was right when it sold that quickly. Any time you are able to get the results you were hoping for, that is a victory. You can always wonder if you could have bought lower and sold higher. But business development done right is finding a way to put together consistent victories, not second-guessing every decision along the way.

EFFECTIVENESS TRUMPS EFFICIENCY

As we've already emphasized, effectiveness trumps efficiency in business development. You don't want to choose the cheapest or the quickest initiative if it doesn't get the results you want, and you don't want to dismiss an initiative just because it doesn't overwhelm you with business immediately. It takes time to fill an empty pipeline, but once you do, you will have new business coming in for a long, long time.

One of our Door Openers® closed a sale and did a very successful project for her new client. After the project she stayed in touch to nurture the relationship so that the client would consider her for more work in the future. It would have been an efficient use of her time to simply call or email him to see if he had another project coming up. That's what most sellers would do. But that would not have been the most effective way for her to grow the relationship. Instead, she got time on his calendar to have a deeper conversation about what she could do that would make his life better and his job easier.

Effectiveness trumps efficiency...

...in business development.

That conversation took more time, but the result was a very large, multifaceted project that he might not have thought of otherwise. He didn't send the project out for a bid; he gave all the work to her without questioning her price. This is an example of choosing effectiveness over efficiency.

Diversifying the Risk of Business Development Initiatives

We mentioned way back in chapter 1 that every business should always have at least five lead-generating activities working simultaneously. Having several different strategies to generate business for your company allows you to hedge against the inevitable ups and downs of any one initiative. If one slows down, another will likely pick right up.

Too many leaders choose just one initiative and end up putting all their eggs in one basket. They may decide that referrals are the best way to grow their businesses, but what will they do when they've exhausted that list of names? On the other hand, if they also have other initiatives going while they're working through the list of referrals, there's a good chance one of those will start generating business when the referrals begin to slow down.

As long as a business development program is paying for itself, it's probably worth keeping. Ideally, you want to have multiple programs that are paying for themselves and bringing in business on a consistent basis. As we said at the beginning of the chapter, finding your unique recipe for lasting business development success is not easy. Most business owners never try enough different things or let the things they do try run long enough to discover it.

So if you've hit on a program with a positive ROI, keep it going. If you decide it's time to replace it, don't terminate it until the replacement program is up and running and outperforming the program you intend to get rid of. You wouldn't quit your old job until you had a new one, so don't cut off a lifeline for your business before the new one is in place.

Carl and I have watched far too many business owners waste millions of dollars when they're on the right track but don't realize it. They hang onto old programs that aren't really delivering, they discontinue a new program before giving it a real chance, or they delay starting an initiative that could bring them real business. They're looking for cheese down all the wrong tunnels instead of systematically analyzing where to find it.

The good news is that if you take the disciplined approach that we've outlined in this chapter, you'll be able to evaluate your choices effectively and judge your results against a realistic timeline. Success becomes inevitable. You'll be able to build and maintain momentum, filling that pipeline. And a full pipeline will guard against even the most challenging market conditions and keep you busy for months and years to come.

CHAPTER 11

GIVING UP

ONE STEP

BEFORE
THE FINISH LINE

– The Perils of Wanting Immediate Gratification.

GIVING UP ONE STEP BEFORE THE FINISH LINE

I magine you're running the Marine Corps Marathon in Washington, DC. You've trained for months, getting up early on countless mornings to log your miles before work. Now it's race day. You've made it through Georgetown, over the bridge, around the Reflecting Pool, and past all the monuments. You're finally headed toward Arlington National Cemetery to that legendary uphill finish.

Even though your heart is pounding, your feet are sore, and your muscles are screaming for oxygen, can you imagine—even for a moment—stopping short of the finish line and saying, "That's enough"? After running over 25 miles, why in the world would you stop before you ran the final 500 feet?

Crossing the finish line in business development often sounds easy in theory. But when sellers don't see results as quickly as they hoped, they can get frustrated, which can cause them to give up just before they achieve success. We've already covered many of the ways business owners give up one step before the finish line. This chapter will review some of those critical mistakes and provide important information on how to avoid them.

By now you should be convinced that doing business development right requires patience and persistence. You must be methodical and deliberate, not allowing setbacks or surprises to distract you from your path to success. But business development is also very dynamic.

When you're doing it right, you are constantly learning from both your successes and your mistakes, perfecting your company's unique recipe. This chapter will teach you how to stay on track, so that you cross that finish line no matter what challenges you face along the way.

GIVING UP ON AN INITIATIVE

As we discussed in the last chapter, many business owners give up on an initiative before it has had the chance to deliver. This can be like paying for your meal at the drive-through but driving off before you get your food: you invest your time and money and get nothing in return.

There can be many tempting reasons to give up on a vendor program or an in-house campaign before you cross the finish line, but most of them have nothing to do with the costs and benefits of the initiative itself. It has more to do with fear. Recently, I was on the phone with an author discussing the publicity efforts for her most recent book. She told me that she had hired a PR agency to promote it and was starting to see activity, but she discontinued their services after just a couple of months. I asked her why, and she responded with a heavy sigh, "I think I looked at the amount of money it was costing every month and got scared. So I just shut it down."

She admitted that, in retrospect, she hadn't given the firm nearly enough time to deliver what they promised. Unfortunately, she spent a lot of money and her time to get the program started but didn't get a return on her investment. Why? Not because the program couldn't deliver but because she didn't give it enough time to deliver. On top of that, she was still stuck with her original problem, which was the need for publicity for her book.

It's very easy to lose confidence in a campaign or initiative for reasons that are almost entirely emotional. The author in this example was an experienced businesswoman, but she made an impulsive decision that hurt her marketing efforts. She gave up just a few steps short of the finish line.

GIVING UP ON A SELLER

As we discussed in chapter 9, it's also easy to give up on sellers before they're able to cross the finish line for your company. I know a business owner who fires any new salesperson who doesn't close a sale in 90 days. He tells them up front that they are being hired for a 90-day trial. At the end of that time, no matter how many high quality prospects they have in the pipeline, he will let them go if they haven't closed a sale.

When I asked him how he came up with this 90-day benchmark, he explained that his best salesperson was able to close her first sale in that period of time. He concluded from this experience that any seller who was capable of delivering what she did would also be able to close a sale in 90 days.

While this reasoning made perfect sense to this business owner, it was flawed for several reasons. First, his best seller might have closed her first sale in 90 days because of luck or because she sold to a friend or family member. That precise circumstance wouldn't necessarily be reproduced in another seller, even if that seller were similarly effective. Second, even if that salesperson were perfect, you wouldn't want to eliminate sellers who were 90 percent as useful as your top performer.

As you can imagine, this business owner has spent a lot of time and money recruiting and training new sellers, only to fire them before they have had a chance to produce. Each time he fires, he's wasting all that time the sellers invested. If he were willing to experiment with increasing the trial period to 120 or even 150 days, what might happen?

The Myth of the Instant Solution

It's easy to read a couple of business books and think that firing someone is synonymous with getting results. Decisive action may be part of good leadership, but just because an action is decisive does not mean it is the right thing to do. Unfortunately, many business owners are convinced that complex problems can be fixed immediately and with one action.

Even the boldest decisions cannot change the underlying reality of your company's natural sales cycle or fix a problem when the cause is something else. The longer your sales cycle, the more patient you need to be with the time it takes your sellers to turn their theoretical training and initial pipeline-building activities into practical results.

How do you guard against giving up on a seller two months before he closes the biggest account you've ever seen? First, be sure the lack of results is not coming from something other than the seller himself. For example, be sure the seller is not being asked to fill his time with non-sales-related activities. This could be one explanation for disappointing results that may have nothing to do with the seller's ability to sell. Second, be sure you're not making a decision during a time when your seller is initiating many new relationships. Expect this part of the sales cycle to be slower to deliver. If you know your own business processes inside out, you can effectively analyze how much a salesperson has in the pipeline. Then you will know whether firing would be cutting dead weight or giving up valuable potential relationships.

GIVING UP ON A PROSPECT

As we discussed way back in chapter 1, you never want to give up on prospects as long as you believe they still meet your criteria for A-level prospects. This means your research shows that they need your product or service in the right quantities for you and will buy in a realistic time frame. This may sound fine in theory, but in daily application it can be challenging for sellers (and their managers) to continue to keep unresponsive prospects in the rotation. After all, at what point do you just throw in the towel? How can you be sure you are spending your time most effectively?

Several years ago, I was getting one of our clients in the door with her wish list prospects, when I came upon the name of a particular prospect on the list. I looked at my notes, which recorded how many times over the past two years I had reached out to this one decision maker.

I am not the type to give up easily, but that day as I looked at those notes, I wondered, "Is this really worth it? Am I really going to leave one more message? What's the point?" But I looked at my original notes describing why I felt this prospect was an "A." I researched a bit to see if there was any new information that would lead me to believe anything had changed. That research only confirmed for me that there was a large opportunity and no reason to stop pursuing this prospect. Out of commitment to my own process, I made that next call. And that was the day that the prospect answered the phone and apologized for not calling me back before. Not only that, he thanked me for my persistence and asked to schedule a time for a meeting.

Had I not called that prospect again, that meeting would never have happened, and the sale would not have closed. Ten years later, that prospect is still a client for my client. It would have been perfectly understandable if I had decided not to make that call, but I would have been giving up one step before the finish line.

You can always think of plenty of reasons not to follow up with a prospect on any given day. Maybe it's the holidays; maybe you've been contacting the prospect for years and haven't heard back. Even experienced sellers can let their heads play tricks on them. They assume prospects have rejected them, when in fact the prospects have just been busy and haven't had time to call back. Stay with it and keep trying, because your competition won't.

Let's take it one step further. Even if your prospect signed with someone else, who says that vendor will do a good job? Think about what else you can provide your prospect with that could get you in the door as a current vendor anyway. Instead of interpreting a proposal that wasn't selected as losing, think of it as "not winning yet."

This mind-set is more than just positive thinking; it is a completely different outlook. If you look at your business development efforts as a work in progress, you understand that "no" almost always means "not now." You see good prospects as either clients now or clients later. You don't give up, because you know you are constantly improving and that circumstances constantly change. For more depth on when to throw in the towel, go to www.BizDevDoneRightBook.com/givingup.com

Overcoming Buyer Obstacles

Sellers aren't the only ones vulnerable to head games; buyers bring their own psychological baggage to the sales process too. Like that steep hill at the end of a long race, you can't let a buyer's emotional resistance cause you to give up a step before the finish line.

Many buyers have made bad purchases in the past and want to protect themselves from making a similar mistake in the future. Others are simply gun shy, so they put hurdle after hurdle in the seller's way to delay the decision. A good seller, however, will learn how to read these signals and respond to them in ways that are both helpful to the buyer and that move the sale forward. Sellers who bring value to the conversation know how to scale those hurdles and make it to the finish line. They can help the prospect refocus on his or her goals and allay any concerns surrounding the purchase.

Remember, business development is ultimately about helping people. **Many of your prospects have been told by their bosses that they must purchase what you sell. They're spending the money; the only question is with whom.** So you are really helping them do their jobs. Are you committed enough to scale that last hurdle and make it to the finish line?

MAKE TIME FOR THE ANALYSIS

Great athletes analyze and learn from every performance. Taking the time to analyze your business development efforts ensures you can constantly improve them. I knew a company that had decided to target a particular vertical market that was brand new to them. As they had their initial conversations and meetings, they learned all sorts of valuable information about that particular niche. This included customer needs as well as what that market could deliver for their bottom line.

Are you committed enough to scale the last hurdle...

...and make it to the finish line?

After the first round of efforts, the company found that they were getting less traction than they had originally hoped for. Instead of giving up, however, they took the time to analyze what was going on. They carefully examined what they learned from their meetings and feedback, and they realized that the real opportunity was in a slightly different market from their original target. So instead of abandoning the whole initiative, they just shifted their target slightly. Then they tested the decision with another round of development efforts, and sure enough, that's where the money was. It took some patience and some careful analysis, but they found a great recipe for success and crossed the finish line.

When you remain objective about what you're doing and commit to learning as much as possible as you do it, you can adjust your strategy to maximize effectiveness. Great business owners are always looking for ways to achieve better results for the time and money invested, so they make time to analyze as they go.

CARL'S COMMENTS:

W. Edwards Deming, an engineer, professor, and management consultant, devised the famous "funnel experiment" to demonstrate how easy it is to make ill-advised adjustments based on just one or two data points. In the experiment, a series of beads are dropped through a funnel with the goal of hitting the center of a target on a paper below. The beads are dropped in various ways in an attempt to manipulate the outcome, and observers notice that adjustments that seem sensible often cause the beads to fall even further away from the center of the target.

The management lesson is this: you have to let a program run, a seller sell, and a prospect percolate for a certain period of time before you conclude that what you're doing is not working. You want your adjustments to be incremental and deliberate, and you want to test them as you go to see if they're having the desired effect.

Deming's experiment is also used to illustrate that there is a certain degree of random variation in life. You can't extrapolate the laws of nature from one or two experiences, or you'll end up firing sellers after 90 days when they may have beaten your best seller if they'd stayed for 120 days. Until you get a certain amount of data, the results you see could be from luck, good or bad. Only after you've collected a large enough pool of data can you start to see some meaningful trends.

Don't Make Decisions Too Soon

Unfortunately, many people try to overhaul their entire process or abandon an initiative after one rejection. If you make large changes the minute something doesn't go well, you are starting all over again rather than learning what's really going wrong. Impulsive decision making leaves you constantly guessing, while methodical decision making leads you to the right changes.

Ask the Right Questions

Before you cut a program, you want to gather all the necessary information. To do this, you need to ask the right questions. For example, you will want to know how the program is delivering compared to the original timeline, but you will also want to determine if the seller is following the system correctly and if anyone else involved has deviated from the system in any way.

Changes in the market and other outside forces can have unanticipated effects, so you'll want to find out if such factors are affecting the program's delivery. Determine what progress has been made and if there are any course corrections that would get it back on track. Lastly, ask yourself if you have given the program sufficient time to deliver or if you are trying to make a decision too soon.

CARL'S COMMENTS:

Years ago, a colleague of mine named David had met with a particular prospect nine times over a year and half. Before he made contact for the tenth, he asked me to sit in on the meeting just to observe. Knowing my friend pretty well, I asked him, "David, would it be okay if we closed the prospect during this meeting?" David laughed and assured me that the prospect was not ready to close but told me I was welcome to try. David had not taken the time to analyze why the meetings hadn't resulted in a closed sale the first nine times. Had he done that he might have been able to course correct and change his approach during his next meeting.

Although David had prepared for a marathon, when I joined him I kept asking questions and heard buying signals in response. Finally, I just explained to the prospect what he was going to get for his investment and assured him we could get started whenever he was ready. And the prospect answered, "That sounds good. Where do I sign?"

Unfortunately, David was so prepared for a marathon that he didn't even have a contract drawn up. So I kept talking to the prospect while David handwrote a brief memorandum of understanding on a legal pad!

Mark the Finish Line in Writing

As basic as it may seem, many companies do not have a written agreement prepared for clients to sign. This is almost like running a race where the finish line is unmarked: you just keep running because you don't know when to stop.

The written document for the close doesn't necessarily have to be a legally binding contract. Depending on your industry, it can be a work agreement, a letter of understanding, an email, or anything that ensures in writing that you and the client are on the same page. Even if there is no legal reason to have the agreement in writing, it is extremely important to the buyer to have something tangible that closes the sale emotionally.

We worked with a professional services firm that didn't have any such closing mechanism. As a result, months would go by between the time their prospects verbally agreed to move forward and the time their work actually began. Sometimes the work wouldn't begin at all. Finally, we showed them on paper how much money they were losing by not having a document that closed the sale and gave a firm start date for their services. Only then did they reconsider their system. It was a simple but important change because it changed the outcome.

CROSSING THE FINISH LINE IS A DAILY DISCIPLINE

The greatest athletes in the world still make time for drills that keep their fundamentals fresh. By now you know you need to research your list of prospects carefully, prepare for each interaction, and take notes on each call and meeting. But in the daily commotion of business development, it's easy to drift away from the things you know you need to do.

The best business owners, sellers, and sales VPs in the world will stay fresh on the fundamentals of business development, but they'll also make mistakes. Many have forgotten to prepare a contract, accidentally sabotaged a meeting, or failed to answer an objection effectively. But the difference between the top performers and everyone else is that top performers learn from their mistakes. They investigate and analyze them until they understand them thoroughly to ensure that they don't repeat them. Everyone else just wants to forget about them as quickly as possible. Keeping your fundamentals fresh and learning from your mistakes are the daily disciplines that ensure you don't give up one step before the finish line.

That finish line is always there, whether it's an initiative, a new seller, or a prospect you've been courting for a couple of years. Keep that finish line in your sights at all times, so you don't give up one step too soon.

CHAPTER 12

BIZ DEV DONE WRONG

– Conclusion/case studies.

BIZ DEV DONE WRONG

Now that we've examined each part of the business development process in great detail, we will end the book with some case studies in business development done wrong. These are situations from all kinds of industries where business owners were struggling with sales for various reasons. Fortunately, most were able to turn things around with relatively minor adjustments.

The key to any solution, as we stated earlier, is correctly pinpointing what is actually going wrong. These stories—drawn from both Carl's and my experiences—demonstrate that problems in the sales process transcend industries, and so do their solutions. You can glean a lot from techniques and strategies that have been applied successfully in a totally different kind of company. In fact, sometimes a fresh perspective is just what the doctor ordered. We trust these examples will help you apply the principles we've discussed so far to your own unique situation.

Caryn: Get the Right Salespeople in the Right Sales Roles

The owner of a contracting company with many field service employees originally called us because he wanted more sales from new customers, and he couldn't understand why he wasn't getting them. After some investigation, we discovered that his seller, "John," was very good at account management, but he just wasn't good at generating new business.

PROSPECT　　　　**SALESPERSON**

Over the years, the owner had tried everything to get John to bring in new accounts—including incentives, micromanagement, and yelling—all to no avail. The owner hired my company to get John the initial meetings with high-level prospects. He figured if he had someone else doing what he considered the hardest part of the business development job, then John might be more successful going on the meetings and closing the sales. As we got John more meetings with his prospects, another problem emerged. John was leaving the meetings without next steps. This problem wasn't evident before, because John wasn't setting enough meetings for anyone to know there was an issue with how he conducted them. We found out by sending one of our Door Openers(r) with him on a few meetings to see what was happening during his interactions with prospects.

John failed to ask "high gain" questions in the beginning of the meeting, which prevented him from uncovering all the opportunities he could have. Further, he wasn't adept at recognizing opportunities either. Because he was mishandling the earlier parts of the meeting, there was little reason for the prospect to agree to a next step. Unfortunately, John was unreceptive to feedback from us or from his management. We determined that John was not a good fit for the company's business development needs, and the owner decided to move him to an account management role.

The business owner, however, wasn't ready to hire any new sellers, because he didn't want to add to his head count. So we took a look at the people he had in-house already. We singled out "Keith" from customer service. Keith was a charismatic communicator and a born problem solver, but he had no sales experience. One of our Door Openers® worked with him to develop a methodical sales system, using all the concepts that we talked about in this book. We taught him how to conduct new prospect meetings and how to close. We continued to get him the meetings with decision makers. His job was to go on the meetings and close the sales.

Within four months, Keith went on twelve new meetings, closed five new accounts, and generated $565,000 of new business. Not bad for a guy who had never been in sales! After he mastered how to structure a meeting that produced an outcome and how to close the sale, we identified an area in which he needed more support. We found that follow-up wasn't his cup of tea. He was disorganized and didn't know what to do to productively nurture relationships after the initial meeting. Instead of teaching him this part of the sales job and making him responsible for it, we determined that because of his innate talents, his time would be better spent going to more meetings and closing more sales. We decided to have our Door Opener® handle the follow-up for any prospects who didn't have an immediate need. Dividing the sales tasks and having each seller do the part that leveraged his or her individual strengths and talents made the sales process significantly more efficient (and enjoyable).

Training Keith in sales and keeping John in account management was exactly what that company needed to accelerate sales growth. They initially thought they just needed more meetings, but they really needed more meetings *and* a personnel shift. These were relatively minor changes that brought about tremendous results. Had we not pointed out the areas in the sales process that were in this business owner's blind spot, he would likely still be struggling to get John to sell today.

Carl: What a Dentist Taught a Financial Services Professional

I worked with a financial services firm in Detroit that lost a great deal of business when the auto industry took a hit in the late 2000's. When we came in to consult, we learned that this firm made money every time a client did a transaction, and as their clients lost money, they did fewer transactions. The company was losing revenue fast, with no end in sight.

We started by asking the owner how often he sat down with his clients to recommend a transaction, and he answered that he always waited for the clients to come to him. "I'm not a sales guy, Carl," he explained. "That's not credible behavior in my industry." I nodded to let him know I understood.

Then I surprised him by asking him to walk me through his last dentist appointment. He thought about it and replied that he got checked in by the receptionist, had his teeth cleaned by the hygienist, and then had his cavity filled by the dentist. The dentist then recommended a few products, which he bought, and then he left with a card for his next appointment.

"So did you feel like the dentist was selling you?" I asked. The business owner realized that his dentist was just giving him good customer service, but he was also securing next appointments with his patients. The owner and I worked to categorize his clientele based on net worth. Then, without putting any additional resources into marketing or sales, he just started setting appointments with his existing clientele. He had an assistant start meeting and greeting the clients, and then he had the junior associate review sections of their portfolios. Then he came in and made the suggestions for any transactions that might benefit them.

This business owner's revenues went up 30 percent, just because he took a page out of his dentist's playbook. More importantly, his clients were happier. They were growing their money faster and felt that they were being serviced better than before.

Caryn: A Minor Adjustment for a Major Breakthrough

Our company worked with a workshop speaker who wanted to do more consulting. She would do a lot of workshops for various companies, but she was having difficulty getting back in the door to discuss follow-up consulting work. This was very problematic for her business, because consulting was much more profitable for her.

At our recommendation, she added one small step to her sales process. When she set the dates and times for her workshops, we also advised her to schedule a management debrief conversation for a week or so after the workshop. Her clients were happy to agree to the debriefing to hear her findings, and this meeting gave her the audience she needed with the decision makers to discuss ongoing consulting work. She offered recommendations based on how she assessed their needs from the workshop, and naturally she was the logical fit to fulfill those recommendations.

Just adding this date and time request for the debriefing after the workshop caused her to get a great deal more consulting work, just as she'd wanted. A small tweak in her sales process brought her a dramatic increase in more profitable revenue.

Carl: It's All about the Small Talk

I worked with a medical device pharmaceutical company that suddenly discovered the importance of sales. For years, they were convinced that their technology was so strong that all they had to do was explain it and service the order. This worked fine, until they got some competition. Their competitors began selling to their weaknesses, pointing out flaws in their system, and eating into their market share. So we were brought in to teach their sales team how to sell.

We soon learned that many of their salespeople had a background in nursing, which meant they understood the technical side of the products very well. But we found that the problem in their sales process was occurring in the "small talk" phase with the prospects, who were mostly doctors. The nurses were so used to addressing doctors as superiors—because that is how it works in the medical field—that the doctors weren't viewing them as authorities on the product they were selling. Even though these salespeople knew every-thing there was to know about the product, they set themselves up in the small talk phase to be dismissed.

So we sat down with these sellers and taught them to address the doctors as equals. We scripted the small talk to help them build their confidence, because we knew if we could get them into the technical side of the discussion, they would flourish. And they did.

The company's sales cycle was about 12 months. When we came to them they had two prospects in the pipeline, and they had closed five clients their best year on record. When we were done coaching their sales team, they had 18 prospects in the pipeline and they closed 9 clients that year. They broke the company record, simply because the sellers overcame the psychological obstacles they had with their prospects.

Caryn: Breaking into New Markets and Leveraging Secret Weapons

The initial interaction with decision makers is absolutely crucial. One of our clients ran a very successful meeting planning company in Europe and wanted to break into the US market with large companies. Before she became a client, she was extremely frustrated because she had had such success overseas, and she couldn't understand what was going wrong with her business development efforts in the states.

She felt like she had tried everything. She attended industry events, created a lengthy newsletter, and made innumerable calls, and yet her first year she closed a paltry $12,000 in sales. When we started working together, we did something she couldn't do for herself: we got her the initial meeting with the high-level decision makers in these large companies. We found that once she was in front of a prospect, something magical happened. She possessed a "secret weapon" for bonding with her prospects: she had stood in the lobbies of thousands of hotels around the world. The people she was meeting with were responsible for planning meetings for their companies and had also seen their share of the same hotel lobbies. So wherever their last conference had been, she had a story or anecdote to relate, and this bond greatly accelerated the relationship.

In the first three years we worked with her, she grew from that $12,000 to $5 million in sales, which came from well-known companies on her ideal client wish list. Her growth wouldn't have been possible had we not gotten the meetings for her and had we not identified as well as leveraged her secret weapon. Sending a different salesperson (who hadn't stood in the lobbies of these hotels) in her place wouldn't have achieved the same results. She just needed us to get her in the door so that she could have the prospect conversations that nobody else could have.

Carl: Sellers versus Closers

We worked with a global training firm whose consultants did most of their selling. As the company grew, their prices went up, and their services became more technology driven. All this gave their sellers a real mental block when it came to closing. They felt like the price point was too high, and they weren't comfortable discussing technological features they didn't fully understand. To add to the confusion, the company had 68 salespeople in 15 different countries, speaking seven different languages.

We found that the majority of the sellers were better at building relationships than they were at closing the deals. So we segmented the sales process based on their skills and identified the best closers in each region. We had most of the salespeople work to determine which prospects were best qualified. Then they would begin building strong relationships. Next, once they got to the decision-making phase, they would automatically introduce them to the closer. The closer would reinforce all the work they had been doing and finish the job. We found that by dividing the work this way, the company's close ratio increased from 13 to 21 percent.

Remember that you have options. You can find the rock star seller who can do all the parts of the sales process very well, although this can be like finding a needle in a haystack. You can find someone who is close in most areas but needs some training, coaching, or incentives. Or you can put together a team of people who are able to complete the process together. The key is to make sure your whole process works efficiently and makes the most of the team you have right now.

Caryn: Don't Fix a Small Problem by Creating a Bigger One

We all know "if it ain't broke, don't fix it," but it's also true that if something isn't very broken, you don't need to overhaul it. Unfortunately, some business owners will respond to a small problem by creating a bigger one.

We were hired by a software development company that was targeting mid-market companies that had ongoing needs for their services. The company was owned by two business partners; one ran the operations, and the other did the selling. The partner who did the selling was very skilled, but she didn't really have time for door opening. So they hired us, and we secured the initial meetings. The selling partner went to the meetings we got for her, built the relationships, and was getting really great traction.

Unfortunately for this company, the selling partner moved overseas and could no longer be part of the sales process. Instead of just replacing her with someone similar, the business owner decided to hire a seller who could take care of all the parts of the sales process. So they hired one person who was supposed to be responsible for "doing it all." He was to find the right prospects, open doors, have the meetings, follow up, get the RFPs, respond to them, and then close the sales. We stopped getting meetings for them, because that was part of the new seller's job.

Three months later, their steady flow of new meetings came to a stop. Their traction faded away. The business owner had several heart-to-heart conversations with this new seller, inquiring after all the new prospect relationships that were in progress when he started. Each time, the seller would promise results, and then there would be a small (and brief) surge in activity. But finally the business owner knew he had to let the seller go.

As it turned out, the new seller was not very good at certain parts of the sales process. Naturally he hadn't said this in his job interview, and the owner hadn't necessarily known what to look for. Although the seller appeared qualified, he neglected certain vital aspects of his job, and the company was left with a lull in activity and an empty pipeline. Worse, the new prospect relationships that the selling owner had started (and the new seller was supposed to nurture) had gone cold.

This owner had a good system in place that was working well. Instead of responding to the loss of one person by overhauling the entire system, he would have been more successful had he sought to replace her with someone of similar capabilities. He ended up losing a lot of time and money unnecessarily.

Carl: Don't Sell, Just Serve

One of our clients was a manufacturer with a very long list of customers whom they sold to periodically. They had been losing revenue and market share every single year since 2008, when the economy took a hit. When they told us they needed new clients, we pointed to their thousands of existing clients and asked why they weren't talking to them on a regular basis.

The owner answered, "We see our clients at all the trade shows. We're constantly talking to them. When they need us, they know to call us." So we challenged them to take one hour a day and start touching base with everyone on their list, one by one. We told them just to ask how business was going, ask about their projects, and ask if there was anything they could help them check off their task lists.

The owners were very skeptical, thinking that their clients wouldn't want to be bothered, but they followed through as we asked. The results were not what they expected. First, they were surprised at how happy their customers were to hear from them. Then, some of those calls started turning into orders, and those orders started to turn into repeat orders.

But something else happened too. They would touch base with a client, and then they would bump into that same person at a trade show a week or two later. They would immediately have something to talk about. Then the trade show conversation would turn into an order. Their business grew 35 percent in 15 months, just because they decided to make courtesy phone calls.

Next level growth requires...

...next level thinking.

Most of the time, it only takes small adjustments to go from biz dev done wrong to Biz Dev Done Right. Everyone has blind spots, so it can be helpful to get an outside opinion to ensure that you fix the right problem. Whether it's finding the missing link in your business development plan or fine-tuning the wording of your sales message, minor changes can bring about major results.

If you've picked up this book, it means you're probably doing many things right. You have a business, you have some sales, and you may even have some salespeople or a large sales team. You have achieved a measure of success and moved beyond Selling 101. You have clients and you have growth. What many business owners, sales VPs, and sellers in this situation struggle with is how to accelerate sales growth.

You've realized you've been doing enough wrong that it has affected your growth and prevented you from achieving your goals. Until now, you didn't know exactly what was wrong or how to fix it. After reading this book, you realize the business development strategies that worked for you before probably won't be the ones that get you to where you want to go now. **Next level growth requires next level thinking.** This book has exposed the key blind spots that prevent many from achieving that next level of growth. Now that you know where to look for your blind spots, you can identify the ones that are getting in your way, fix them, and clear the path to the cash.

A Note from Carl and Caryn:

We hope you enjoyed this book and will keep us posted on your successes. Visit us at www.BizDevDoneRightBook.com to learn more, access more resources, and connect with other like-minded business development professionals.

Notes and Brilliant Ideas

_____

_____

_____

_____

_____

_____

_____

_____

_____

_____

_____

_____

_____

Notes and Brilliant Ideas

Notes and Brilliant Ideas

Notes and Brilliant Ideas

Notes and Brilliant Ideas

Notes and Brilliant Ideas

Notes and Brilliant Ideas

_____

_____

_____

_____

_____

_____

_____

_____

_____

_____

_____

_____

Notes and Brilliant Ideas

Notes and Brilliant Ideas

Notes and Brilliant Ideas

Notes and Brilliant Ideas

Notes and Brilliant Ideas

CORE COLLECTION 2015